CESAR CHAVEZ

CESAR CHAVEZ

Other titles in the
People Who Made History series:

PEOPLE
WHO MADE
HISTORY

CESAR CHAVEZ

Michelle E. Houle, *Book Editor*

Daniel Leone, *President*
Bonnie Szumski, *Publisher*
Scott Barbour, *Managing Editor*
David M. Haugen, *Series Editor*

GREENHAVEN
PRESS®

THOMSON
———✳———
GALE

San Diego • Detroit • New York • San Francisco • Cleveland
New Haven, Conn. • Waterville, Maine • London • Munich

LIBRARY OF CONGRESS CATALOGING-IN-PUBLICATION DATA

Cesar Chavez / Michelle E. Houle, book editor.
p. cm. — (People who made history)
Includes bibliographical references and index.
ISBN 0-7377-1299-6 (pbk. : alk. paper) — ISBN 0-7377-1298-8 (lib. : alk. paper)
1. Chavez, Cesar, 1927– . 2. Migrant agricultural laborers—Labor unions—United States—Officials and employees—Biography. 3. Labor leaders—United States—Biography. I. Houle, Michelle E. II. Series.
HD6509.C48 C47 2003
331.88'13'092—dc21
2002027152

Printed in the United States of America

4353

CONTENTS

Chapter 1: The First Struggles

After the repossession of the Chavez family farm, which left them without a home or means of income, the family searched for work as migrant laborers. Episodes of unlawful discrimination combined with long hours of injurious work informed Chavez's crusade against prejudice.

Lax enforcement of child labor laws meant many underage workers labored in the fields. Even with the income earned by the Chavez children, the family struggled for subsistence.

Chavez rebelled against the institutions that oppressed his community. When he decided to take action, such as protesting segregation, he landed in jail.

In their quest for work, the Chavez family moved to the San Jose barrio of *Sal Si Puedes*, literally "get out if you can." It was there that Chavez got involved with community organization and eventually built his first union.

Chavez envisioned a union that would not only raise wages and living conditions for farm laborers but could also function as a catalyst for social change. Four months after the beginning of the Delano grape strike, Chavez made progress toward this goal.

Chapter 2: The Social and Political Impact of Chavez's Work

Chavez's arrest and imprisonment as a result of the 1970 United Farm Workers lettuce boycott provoked mass demonstrations, and humanitarians such as Coretta Scott King and Ethel Kennedy rallied to his cause. The extent of Chavez's committment made others in the movement reflect on the power and meaning behind the labor struggle.

Chapter 3: Strategies and Tactics of an Organizer

Chapter 4: The Legacy of Cesar Chavez

FOREWORD

In the vast and colorful pageant of human history, a handful of individuals stand out. They are the men and women who have come variously to be called "great," "leading," "brilliant," "pivotal," or "infamous" because they and their deeds forever changed their own society or the world as a whole. Some were political or military leaders—kings, queens, presidents, generals, and the like—whose policies, conquests, or innovations reshaped the maps and futures of countries and entire continents. Among those falling into this category were the formidable Roman statesman/general Julius Caesar, who extended Rome's power into Gaul (what is now France); Caesar's lover and ally, the notorious Egyptian queen Cleopatra, who challenged the strongest male rulers of her day; and England's stalwart Queen Elizabeth I, whose defeat of the mighty Spanish Armada saved England from subjugation.

Some of history's other movers and shakers were scientists or other thinkers whose ideas and discoveries altered the way people conduct their everyday lives or view themselves and their place in nature. The electric light and other remarkable inventions of Thomas Edison, for example, revolutionized almost every aspect of home-life and the workplace; and the theories of naturalist Charles Darwin lit the way for biologists and other scientists in their ongoing efforts to understand the origins of living things, including human beings.

Still other people who made history were religious leaders and social reformers. The struggles of the Arabic prophet Muhammad more than a thousand years ago led to the establishment of one of the world's great religions—Islam; and the efforts and personal sacrifices of an American reverend named Martin Luther King Jr. brought about major improvements in race relations and the justice system in the United States.

Each anthology in the People Who Made History series begins with an introductory essay that provides a general overview of the individual's life, times, and contributions. The group of essays that follow are chosen for their accessibility to a young adult audience and carefully edited in consideration of the reading and comprehension levels of that audience. Some of the essays are by noted historians, professors, and other experts. Others are excerpts from contemporary writings by or about the pivotal individual in question. To aid the reader in choosing the material of immediate interest or need, an annotated table of contents summarizes the article's main themes and insights.

Each volume also contains extensive research tools, including a collection of excerpts from primary source documents pertaining to the individual under discussion. The volumes are rounded out with an extensive bibliography and a comprehensive index.

Plutarch, the renowned first-century Greek biographer and moralist, crystallized the idea behind Greenhaven's People Who Made History when he said, "To be ignorant of the lives of the most celebrated men of past ages is to continue in a state of childhood all our days." Indeed, since it is people who make history, every modern nation, organization, institution, invention, artifact, and idea is the result of the diligent efforts of one or more individuals, living or dead; and it is therefore impossible to understand how the world we live in came to be without examining the contributions of these individuals.

Introduction: A Commitment to Civil Rights

Cesar Chavez changed the face of American agricultural labor. In his career as an advocate for the often-disenfranchised migrant worker, Chavez helped hundreds of thousands of people make significant gains in their quests for improvement in health and safety conditions. But he was more than a labor leader. He was a pivotal advocate for civil rights. Chavez's philosophy of nonviolence led to comparisons with Dr. Martin Luther King Jr. and Indian activist Mohandas Gandhi. His decisions to fast as a means of nonviolent protest underscored his commitment to sacrifice and added a religious dimension to his struggle. These acts also attached an air of mysticism to the man that at times threatened to overshadow his deeds.

His labor accomplishments were significant and concrete. Chavez established a union for farmworkers where there had been none. His National Farm Workers Association merged with the Agricultural Workers Organizing Committee, which eventually became the United Farm Workers of America (UFW). The UFW won crucial benefits for its constituency, including mandatory rest periods, clean drinking water, access to lavatory facilities, and the prohibition of *el cortito*—an agricultural hoe responsible for crippling workers with its backbreakingly awkward, short handle. Chavez continued to lead boycotts and campaigns throughout his life, gaining both supporters and enemies along the way.

Chavez's critics called him power hungry and manipulative. Some accused him of cultivating an ambiguous movement instead of growing a union. But the vast majority of historians consider Chavez's contribution to labor reform substantial, his legacy of civil rights activism profound. According to historians Matt S. Meier and Feliciano Rivera, "Whatever criticism may be leveled at his activities, [Chavez]

must be given credit for bringing the benefits of union organization to the last large segment of unorganized American
labor. . . . He was the first Chicano to achieve national recognition through his farm worker organizational activities and
has become a national unifying force for Chicanos from
quite diverse social and economic levels."[1] Chavez is remembered for both his monumental contributions to organized labor and his intense, lifelong commitment to the civil
rights movement.

FROM THE HACIENDA TO THE FARM

In the latter part of the nineteenth century, many Mexican
families immigrated to California to escape the bloody Mexican revolution. Others fled the desperate poverty of the
oppressive hacienda system. In this system, *hacendados,* or
plantation owners, trapped Mexican workers into indentured servitude, condemning them to a life of ever-
escalating debt. The United States, however, was not kind to
the immigrants. While it was true that Mexican workers
could earn higher wages in the United States, often U.S. employers exploited this fact to keep wages comparatively low.

Cesario Chavez, Cesar's grandfather, joined the flow of
immigrants to the United States from Chihuahua, Mexico, in
the 1880s to escape the hardships of the hacienda and start
a new life for his family. He moved to El Paso, Texas, and
eventually settled on a farm in the Gila River valley near
Yuma, Arizona. Cesario, or Papa Chayo as he was called,
homesteaded a farm near Yuma with his wife, Dorotea, and
their fifteen children.

Their son Librado married a woman by the name of
Juana Estrada, an émigré from Chihuahua, Mexico. On
March 31, 1927, Cesar Estrada Chavez was born to Librado
and Juana Chavez on the family farm. Librado and Juana
had six children, Cesar being the oldest son. The family
farmed and worked the land, and eventually Librado became something of an entrepreneur. He started several businesses, including a grocery store, pool hall, and garage. At
one point he was elected town postmaster.

Cesar Chavez has said that his early years were some of
the happiest times in his life. According to labor historian
Cletus E. Daniel, "Chavez enjoyed during his youth the kind
of close and stable family life that farmworkers caught in the
relentless currents of the western migrant stream longed for

but rarely attained."[2] Although the support of his close-knit family provided Cesar with pleasant memories of his childhood on the family farm, disaster was looming.

A MORAL EDUCATION

On October 24, 1929, the stock market crash precipitated the worldwide financial catastrophe known as the Great Depression. Millions of dispossessed Americans headed to California in search of work. While the effects of the depression did not discriminate, certain groups of migrants faced additional misfortunes. In California and Arizona, ethnic segregation was enforced in restaurants, theaters, schools, and many public facilities. Non-Anglo migrants were frequently victims of institutionalized racism. The reality of migrant work during the depression was arduous labor for minuscule wages, and little or no hope for escaping desperate poverty. For non-Anglo migrant workers, these hardships were compounded by ethnic discrimination and exploitation. Despite the need for work, some Hispanic migrants did take a stand against the oppression. There were a number of farmworker strikes in the late 1920s and early 1930s held by unhappy Mexican laborers who worked California fields. Worker strikes occurred in strawberry, pea, cotton, and fruit fields in 1933 alone. But the resistance was not organized, and few long-lasting goals were achieved.

The large and close-knit community who patronized Librado's businesses initially cushioned the Chavezes from economic disaster. Librado and Juana continued the tradition of farming and living off the land, and they took seriously the moral education of their children. Cesar learned from his mother the tenets of nonviolence and charity through her *dichos* and *cuentos,* sayings and morality tales that instilled a sense of social and spiritual responsibility in Cesar from a young age. Some of her sayings, such as "It takes two to fight" and "Turn the other cheek" had an impact on Cesar's nonviolent philosophy. Cesar's mother chose St. Eduvigis, a former duchess who gave all her belongings to charity, as her patron saint. Juana maintained an open-door policy to anyone requiring assistance, and each year she commemorated St. Eduvigis's holy day by seeking out others to help. This was not the only type of education Cesar had, however. In the Southwest at this time, traditional schools were plagued with the same race hatred that infected society. White students and teachers created a hostile environment for non-Anglo children. Cesar attended schools where children were punished and ridiculed for speaking Spanish. He later wrote, "When we spoke Spanish, the teacher swooped down on us. I remember the ruler whistling through the air as its edge came down sharply across my knuckles."[3] This experience gave Cesar a deeper understanding of how inferior Mexican American migrants were made to feel in the West.

CATASTROPHIC CHANGES

In the 1930s, severe drought plagued fields in the southern and western United States. The parched land became impossible to farm, and the top layers of soil, loosened by the lack of vegetation, created tumultuous dust storms that blew across the land like black tornadoes. As the frequency and severity of the dust storms increased, crops were destroyed and families were forced to leave their homes. The collective phenomena became known as the Dust Bowl, in which hundreds of thousands of displaced workers struggled to survive. The unemployed laborers, from a variety of ethnic backgrounds, headed west looking for work, and in doing so created a massive labor pool ripe for exploitation.

Migrants from the Dust Bowl now competed with the Mexican American migrant workers for the same miserable jobs. Workers from all backgrounds frequently encountered unethical hiring practices and wage manipulation at the hands of corrupt growers and labor contractors. Most labor camps in the West were nightmares, miserable shanties often lacking water, cooking facilities, and bathrooms. The migrants, however, had little power to better their situation. In 1935, the National Labor Relations Act was passed, guaranteeing many workers organizing and collective bargaining rights. But for the laborers in the fields, real benefits from this law were nonexistent. In fact, to appease the powerful agricultural voting bloc, farm laborers had been specifically excluded from the benefits of the new law.

On August 29, 1937, a bank loan default led to the repossession of the Chavez family property, and they were given one year to vacate the premises. The Chavezes lost their home, farm, and all Librado's businesses. Papa Chayo had died several years earlier but had left a small house for his wife. With few options, the family moved in to Papa Chayo's adobe home and stayed with Cesar's grandmother, whom the family called Mama Tella. Mama Tella was a deeply religious Roman Catholic who educated her children and grandchildren with nightly Bible lessons. From their grandmother, the Chavez children would learn enough Catholic history to fulfill church requirements for taking first communion.

Losing the family home was traumatic enough, but the sight of the new owner gleefully bulldozing cherished trees and family structures made a lasting impression on young Cesar Chavez. Broke, homeless, and unemployed, the Chavezes left Mama Tella's with what they could and headed west. Cesar recalled, "When we were pushed off our land, all we could take with us was what we could jam into the old Studebaker or pile on its roof and fenders, mostly clothes and bedding. . . . Our whole life was upset, turned upside down."[4]

By the fall of 1939, a substantial amount of rain fell, bringing an end to the catastrophic drought. The Chavezes had left Arizona to work as migrant laborers. As they followed the crops, Cesar learned from his father about the existence of labor unions. On many occasions he accompanied his father to strike meetings. Rather than suffer injustices, Librado would quit abusive jobs when he encountered them, which made a huge impression on Cesar. He recalled, "I don't want to suggest we were that radical, but I know we were probably one of the strikingest families in California. . . . We were constantly fighting against things that most people would probably accept because they didn't have that kind of life we had in the beginning, that strong family life and family ties which we would not let anyone break. . . . Our dignity meant more than money."[5]

PACHUCO REBEL

On December 7, 1941, the Japanese bombed Pearl Harbor and the United States entered World War II. Mexican Americans enlisted in large numbers to join the war effort. At the outset of the war, the Chavezes worked seasonal crops, including grape vineyards and lettuce fields, and were often forced to use *el cortito*, the torturous short-handled hoe, in their work. Within a few months, Librado was injured in a car accident, and the family's financial troubles forced Cesar to quit school and work full-time to support his family. After attending more than thirty different schools, Cesar had managed to graduate from the eighth grade. The war effort had produced a shortage of hired hands on many farms, and to combat this, in 1942, Congress enacted the Bracero Program. *Braceros* referred to Mexican laborers, and the program brought in 5 million Mexican farmworkers to work the fields. Although conceived as a war relief effort, the Bracero Program remained in effect until 1965 because the Mexican workers accepted low pay and did not unionize for fear of losing their jobs.

During this period, an outlet for frustrated teens was to dress in a manner that disturbed established norms. The zoot suit, an oversized jacket paired with pegged baggy pants, was seen by conservative Mexican and Anglo Americans as a rebellious fashion. The young men who wore them were called *pachucos*. People caught wearing the distinctive style of a pachuco ran the risk of being stereotyped as rabble-rousers or thugs. "I started wearing zoot suits when it became an issue," Cesar Chavez told *Lowrider* magazine. "The Chicano community was divided about the dress. Some people just wouldn't wear them, because they thought everybody who did was no good. . . . You see, the people that wore them *eran los mas pobres* [were the poorest], guys like us who were migrant farm workers."[6]

Then in August 1942, a young man named José Diaz was found beaten to death near a reservoir nicknamed Sleepy Lagoon. Police rounded up over six hundred "zoot suiters" and other migrants, while California newspapers sensationalized distortions of facts about the crime. Seventeen youths were charged, and during the trial, the defendants' civil rights were systematically violated. This mockery of justice contributed to both an anti-Mexican sentiment on the part of many Anglo Americans, and a Mexican American distrust of the legal system. Two years later the verdicts were overturned, and all seventeen suspects were released with cleared records. But the damage had already been done. Bloody race riots known as the "Zoot Suit Riots," in which racist marauders brutalized Chicanos and African Americans, erupted in 1943. This mob violence, along with the Sleepy Lagoon debacle, made a deep impression on Cesar and his friends. The Chavez family relocated to Delano, California, where Cesar's anger at these events would eventually help influence his decision to join the Community Service Organization.

RITES OF PASSAGE

In 1943 Delano was a town divided. Restaurants and movie theaters segregated their patrons into Anglos and non-Anglos by means of verbal intimidation and signs. Postings such as "No Dogs or Mexicans Allowed" were common. In 1944 Chavez violated the segregation policy of his local movie theater by sitting in the "whites only" section. He was arrested, taken to police headquarters, and detained for approximately an hour. The experience changed Chavez. Biographers Richard Griswold del Castillo and Richard A. Garcia note, "Cesar learned that segregation was an evil, making people feel excluded and inferior. As a result, one of the main tenets of his later organizing philosophy was that neither racial nor ethnic prejudice had a place within a farm workers' union movement."[7]

Later the same year, after his seventeenth birthday, Chavez joined the navy and served in the Pacific fleet. His tour of duty took him through Guam and Saipan. Chavez hated naval life. He credits his experience in the navy with enlightening him to the fact that minority groups other than Mexicans suffered racism as well.

In 1946, Chavez received his discharge from the navy and returned to Delano, California, to resume work in the vineyards. According to historians Meier and Rivera, "World War II had made [Chicanos] aware of their political and economic rights as American citizens and conscious of widespread denial of those rights. Returning to their communities, they found themselves still limited to the poorest-paying jobs and to the most dilapidated housing and with only limited access to education and other public services."[8] Having received no specialized training from the navy, Chavez returned to the only work he knew—field labor.

On October 22, 1948, Cesar Chavez married Helen Fabela, whom he had met when he was fifteen years old. Helen had worked in a service station, in a Delano ice cream parlor, and at times as a migrant worker. The newlyweds spent their honeymoon traveling south from Sonoma to San Diego, visiting each of the historic California missions. Their first child, Fernando, was born in 1949. Eventually, the Chavezes would have eight children: Sylvia (1950), Linda (1951), Eloise (1952), Ana (1953), Paul (1957), Elizabeth (1958), and Anthony (1958).

COMMUNITY ACTIVIST

In 1952 Chavez and his family moved to the San Jose barrio known as *Sal Si Puedes* (literally, "get out if you can"). He found a job at a lumber mill where he worked with his brother Richard. In this rundown neighborhood, Chavez met two people who were to become influential figures in his life: Father Donald McDonnell and Fred Ross. Father McDonnell ministered to the local residents from his small barrio church and introduced Chavez to the history of Catholic involvement in activist movements. He educated Chavez on the history of organized labor and acquainted him with historical servants of the underclass such as St. Francis of Assisi and Indian nonviolence activist Mohandas Gandhi.

Fred Ross was a member of Saul Alinsky's Community Service Organization (CSO). The mission of the CSO was to empower people of depressed communities through programs such as voter registration drives and legal aid. After Chavez got over his reluctance to meet with this Anglo "outsider," he found that Ross was well versed in the recent histories of labor and racial injustices. Ross successfully recruited Chavez into the CSO in 1952. As part of his service, Chavez spearheaded voter registration drives and held "house meetings." House meetings worked like a chain reaction: An organizer would set up a meeting in a person's home and ask him to invite his friends and coworkers and then explain what the CSO hoped to accomplish. They concluded the meetings by recruiting interested parties to hold subsequent meetings in different homes. Chavez was an effective recruiter, and his relationship with the CSO would continue for ten more years.

Also in 1952, Congress enacted the McCarran-Walter Act, commonly known as the Immigration and Nationality Act. This law created quotas of how many immigrants from particular nationalities were to be allowed to enter the country. The new policy reflected a growing anti-immigration sentiment in the United States, and the continued presence of the braceros only seemed to compound the problem. The Immigration and Naturalization Service (INS) launched a campaign, "Operation Wetback," to deport undocumented Mexican workers. Chavez and the CSO protested this campaign, which was intended to alleviate increased illegal immigration along the Mexican-American border but in practice routinely combed Mexican neighborhoods in cities far from the border for identification checks on people who "looked Mexican."

Chavez's involvement with the CSO, particularly his success at registering voters, had not gone unnoticed by his political enemies. To sully his name, opponents ran a newspaper ad that accused Chavez of having Communist ties. This attack coincided with the Red Scare paranoia of the era, which had been ushered in by Senator Joseph McCarthy and other political conservatives. Chavez denied any involvement with communism, and explained to anyone who asked that he had no interest in anything Communist.

CIVIL RIGHTS AT ISSUE

On May 17, 1954, the *Brown v. Board of Education* decision rendered racial segregation in public schools unconstitutional. Civil rights leaders such as Martin Luther King Jr. gained more public recognition as their efforts to end discrimination attracted national attention. Hispanic Americans, who also suffered civil rights abuses, did not yet have a visible figurehead to draw attention to their plight. Chavez hoped that his work with the CSO might help bring at least the injustices suffered by farmworkers to the attention of influential politicians.

In 1958, the CSO promoted Chavez to general director. He was asked to establish a chapter in Oxnard, California, to assist citrus-packing workers in their efforts. Among other issues, Chavez applied pressure to the growers who violated the law by hiring braceros when a supply of American laborers was available. The CSO was successful in reforming this policy in Oxnard, and the organization grew with each victory. As director, Chavez required commitments of nonviolence from his volunteer recruits. He saw this as crucial in his effort to promote civil rights as well as labor gains. Chavez's commitment to nonviolent protest became an integral part of his life philosophy. In 1959, to discuss voter registration, social issues, and the civil rights of farmworkers, Chavez met with Robert Kennedy, who was then a lawyer for the Senate committee on labor activities. Through his investigations into union actions and alleged violations of workers' rights, Kennedy helped pass the Labor Reform Act of 1959. Chavez and Kennedy began a close relationship that they would maintain throughout their careers.

The public eye became increasingly focused on race relations and civil rights issues in the early 1960s. On February 1, 1960, sit-ins were held in Greensboro, North Carolina, to protest segregation. On April 15, the Student Nonviolent Coordinating Committee (SNCC) was established to organize civil rights protesters. And in November of the same year, CBS aired Edward R. Murrow's "Harvest of Shame," an exposé of the grueling workload and economic hardships suffered by American migrant workers.

A UNION OF HIS OWN

On March 31, 1962, Chavez resigned from the CSO in a dispute over the organization's unwillingness to charter a union specifically for farmworkers. The family moved back to Delano. Dolores Huerta, an activist and labor lobbyist who had been involved with the CSO for seven years, shared Chavez's desire to organize farmworkers and left the CSO to join him. On September 30, Chavez and Huerta established the National Farm Workers Association (NFWA) at their founding convention in Fresno, California. Huerta became the union's cofounder and first vice president. At the Fresno convention, the pair unveiled the distinctive flag that would come to symbolize the entire movement: a black Aztec eagle in a white circle on a red background. An editorial newspaper, *El Malcriado* (the Bad Boy), was also founded. Its political cartoons, satirical essays, and commentaries on union activities provided unique recordings of the lives of the readership.

In 1963, Chavez refused a well-paying job with the Peace Corps in Latin America to concentrate on building his fledgling union. For all practical purposes, Helen handled the day-to-day duties of raising their children. But sometimes the children rode along with their father as he spent long hours driving through fields, meeting with farmworkers, and recruiting new union members. Chavez knew that building a union would be a slow, painstaking project, and his livelihood partly depended on the charity of those he hoped to organize. On his NFWA recruiting drives, he slept at the migrant workers' homes and ate whatever they were able to feed him. During his entire career, he never accepted more than a $5,000 annual salary.

STRIKE!

While the NFWA continued to build its membership, other unions actively continued their work on farm labor issues.

One of the largest, composed mainly of Filipino workers, was led by Larry Itilong. Itilong's Agricultural Workers Organizing Committee (AWOC) members were unhappy with the low wages and oppressive working conditions in the vineyards of Delano. To protest a lack of willingness to negotiate on the part of the larger growers, on September 8, 1965, they held a strike. They refused to work and instead carried picket signs denouncing the growers' antibargaining positions. Chavez and the NFWA faced a dilemma. He was not convinced that his fledgling union had a solid enough membership base to carry out a sustained strike against a wealthy conglomerate of grape growers. But many NFWA members worked in the Delano vineyards, were also dissatisfied with their pay and employment conditions, and felt allegiances to their fellow AWOC coworkers. Chavez decided to hold a vote on the strike issue, and the members of the NFWA agreed overwhelmingly to join AWOC in the strike. On September 16, Mexican Independence Day, the NFWA officially joined what would come to be known as the Great Delano Grape Strike.

Striking workers met with tough and often violent resistance to their actions. Robert Kennedy traveled to Delano to investigate attacks on picketers and unlawful arrests by police who were sympathetic to the growers. To draw attention to their strike, on March 16, 1966, Chavez led supporters on a three-hundred-mile march from Delano to the state capital, Sacramento. Expanded media attention and a signed contract with Schenley Vineyards, one of the major grape growers, were achieved as a result of this pilgrimage. But there were many other contracts to sign before the massive strike could be resolved. To strengthen the movement, in August 1966, the AWOC and NFWA merged. Together, they formed the United Farm Workers Organizing Committee (later renamed the United Farm Workers of America, or UFW), and Chavez was named director. The next year, the UFW discovered that Giumarra Vineyards, a target of the strike, had been using labels purchased from other growers to bypass the damage incurred by the boycotts. In response, Chavez extended the boycott to all California-grown table grapes. Chavez and the UFW found themselves in battles on multiple fronts. A rapidly increasing problem soon became a territorial dispute with the Teamsters Union.

The Teamsters were an alliance of truck drivers and industrial workers led at the time by controversial figure Jimmy Hoffa. The Teamsters engaged growers in secret "sweetheart deals" that would designate the Teamsters as the official union for that particular grower's employees. These deals were so named because of the mutually beneficial terms that aided growers by short-changing workers on benefits they would have received from the UFW and increasing the number of dues-paying Teamsters. The picket lines became increasingly more violent. Striking UFW members were threatened and victimized by hired Teamster thugs. While attempting to negotiate a truce with Bill Grami, the lead organizer for the agricultural branch of the Teamsters, Chavez embarked on his first of many fasts. According to historians Richard Griswold del Castillo and Richard A. Garcia, "[Chavez] had been praying for a satisfactory resolution to the talks and, when victory appeared imminent, he had decided to observe a fast of thanksgiving. The purpose of the fast changed, however, when the negotiations stalled. It was now undertaken as a protest."[9] Chavez continued to fast for thirteen days to pray for a peaceful resolution to the turf war with the Teamsters. The whole experience left him weak and drained for days.

The Great Grape Strike continued and the UFW experienced an extended period of membership growth in 1967. It relocated its headquarters to Delano, into an office complex known as "Forty Acres." On February 14, 1968, with progress in the strike seemingly stalled, Chavez staged another fast to draw attention to the strike. He fasted for twenty-five days. Dr. Martin Luther King Jr. sent a telegram to Chavez. It read, "As brothers in the fight for equality, I extend the hand of fellowship and good will and wish continuing success to you and your members. . . . You and your valiant fellow workers have demonstrated your commitment to righting grievous wrongs forced upon exploited people. We are together with you in spirit and in determination that our dreams for a better tomorrow will be realized."[10] Senator Robert Kennedy broke bread with Chavez at a special mass held to celebrate the end of the fast. In a speech from the mass, he called Chavez "one of the heroic figures of our time."[11] Sadly, both King and Kennedy would be assassinated before the year was out, depriving Chavez of two friends and fellow activists. However, other politicians and religious leaders lent public support to Chavez, and national media coverage drew a tremendous amount of attention to both the strike and the plight of the farmworkers in general.

On May 10, 1969, Chavez marched in Indio, California, to protest the use of undocumented workers as strikebreakers. The march lasted nine days and attracted a wide range of supporters, from senators to Hollywood stars. Reporter Jacques E. Levy began to travel with Chavez in order to document the turbulence, keeping a notebook that later became a work titled *Cesar Chavez: An Autobiography of La Causa.* It is a fascinating montage of news articles, testimonials, and documentation of violence, detentions, and arrests.

On July 29, 1970, almost five years after the workers first picked up their picket signs, contracts with twenty-eight grape growers, including Giumarra Vineyards, were signed. Even though their victory was five years in the making, the time to celebrate was short lived. The Teamsters had decided to reenergize their campaign against the UFW.

NEW AND REEMERGING PROBLEMS

While Chavez and the UFW had concentrated their energies on the grape problem, many lettuce and vegetable growers, unhappy with the UFW, signed contracts with the Teamsters. In response, Chavez targeted lettuce crops as the union's next boycott effort. On December 14, Chavez was jailed in Salinas, California, as a result of his refusal to call an end to the boycott against one grower in particular, Bud Antle Lettuce. Chavez's imprisonment provoked vigils and mass demonstrations, and he received visits from several prominent figures, including Ethel Kennedy, the widow of Robert Kennedy, and Coretta Scott King, the widow of Martin Luther King Jr. Chavez was released from jail on December 24. The lettuce boycott would continue until 1978.

In 1971, Chavez and the UFW acquired a converted tuberculosis sanitorium and created a new headquarters near Keene, California. They named it *"La Paz"* (the Peace). Meanwhile, Chavez faced pressures from all directions. In 1972, agribusiness and political conservatives lobbied for Arizona Proposition 22, which would outlaw labor boycotts. Chavez went to Phoenix and began another fast, this time to protest anti-union legislation such as Proposition 22. The fast lasted for twenty-four days, and the proposition was defeated. This victory marked a high point in union strength. Membership reached new levels and the UFW became an official affiliate of the powerful American Federation of Labor and Congress of Industrial Organizations (AFL-CIO). The next year, a UFW convention was held in Fresno at which Senator Edward Kennedy spoke and a constitution was ratified.

But in early 1973 bloody turf wars had reerupted between the UFW and the Teamsters (interestingly, both were now AFL-CIO affiliates). The Teamsters were holding secret negotiations with one of the largest growers, the Gallo Winery, in an effort to oust UFW contracts. On June 27, to protest dealings with the Teamsters Union, Chavez announced a strike on the Gallo Vineyards. On February 22, 1975, the Gallo boycott was energized with a march on Modesto, California. Newly elected governor Jerry Brown joined the march. Two years later, a truce was finally negotiated between the UFW and the Teamsters. The Gallo boycott, however, lasted until 1978.

VICTORIES

Chavez and the UFW had a staunch ally in Governor Brown. Together, they worked on creating meaningful legal advances for the community of California migrant workers. In March 1975 the California Supreme Court outlawed *el cortito*, the cruel, short-handled hoe that had caused many back injuries to farm laborers. In California that May, under the direct supervision of Governor Brown with input from Chavez, the Labor Relations Act was passed, and the Agricultural Labor Relations Board (ALRB) was formed. The Agricultural Labor Relations Act, nicknamed the California bill of rights for farmworkers, is a law designed to prohibit unfair labor practices. It requires a five-person board to officiate secret-ballot elections of union officials, provides for swift and timely elections, and guarantees that a worker may not be terminated because of membership in a particular union. It also asserts collective bargaining rights for unions. These victories were significant achievements for Chavez and his thirteen-year-old union.

MOMENTUM IS LOST

In 1978, after a few new contracts were signed, Chavez and the UFW decided to drop generalized product boycotts in lieu of boycotts against individual labels. The next year, Marshall Ganz, UFW chief attorney Jerry Cohen, and several other prominent union members decided to leave the organization. Their reasons for quitting the union varied, but their defections spurred media speculation that Chavez was losing his grip on the movement. Some of the staff who resigned were upset with perceived nepotism, others with Chavez's management style. The press captured the shake-up, and the bad publicity decreased membership. Chavez ordered an internal restructuring.

The next five years marked a downward trend in terms of union contracts and membership. Republican governor George Deukmejian, the candidate supported by agricultural conglomerates, did not share former governor Brown's desire to see the UFW succeed. He appointed candidates to the Agricultural Labor Relations Board who were adversarial, if not outright hostile, to the UFW. As a result, complaints made to the board by the UFW were often deferred in such a way that the union's clout was rendered practically impotent. In 1984, Chavez and the UFW declared a new boycott on grapes. In spite of the internal problems and decreasing membership, Chavez gave one of his more eloquent and profound speeches. He said, "Once social change begins, it cannot be reversed. You cannot uneducate the person who has learned to read. You cannot humiliate the person who feels pride. You cannot oppress the people who are not afraid anymore. . . . And [as] you cannot do away with an entire people, you cannot stamp out a people's cause. Regardless of what the future holds for the union, regardless of what the future holds for farm workers, our accomplishments cannot be undone."[12]

FINAL BATTLES

In 1987, *The Wrath of Grapes,* a polemic movie about the poisoning of farmworkers by the unmonitored use of crop pesticides, was produced by the UFW. Chavez screened the movie across the country and led a campaign to ban hazardous chemicals such as DDT and increase awareness of pesticide dangers. On July 16, 1988, Chavez fasted for thirty-six days. He described his motivations for the fast: "I have been studying the plague of pesticides. . . . The evil is far greater than even I had thought it to be. . . . [The] solution to this deadly crisis will not be found in the arrogance of the powerful, but in solidarity with the weak and helpless. I pray to God that this fast will be a preparation for a multitude of simple deeds for justice."[13] Historians del Castillo and Garcia note, "As in the past, the fast became a rallying point for union supporters. Daily bulletins on Cesar's health were issued . . . and nightly mass was held, with thousands in attendance."[14] Celebrities, activists, and politicians once again expressed solidarity with Chavez, and Reverend Jesse Jackson attended the break of the fast.

On November 12, 1990, Chavez was awarded the Aztec Eagle, the highest civilian honor, from the president of Mexico. His celebrity was riding high, but the union was in decline. In 1991 the UFW received a potentially devastating blow when it lost two lawsuits filed by growers. The union was ordered to pay $1.1 million to Daggio, Inc., and $5.4 million to Bruce Church, Inc., for damages incurred during the boycott. The UFW appealed the verdicts. Chavez stayed with a friend in San Luis, Arizona, a small town relatively close to his birthplace, while he testified for the union against the lawsuits. On April 23, 1993, after two days of examination by attorneys for Bruce Church, Chavez died in his sleep.

SOCIAL LEADER

Cesar Chavez's sudden death shocked and devastated many. More than forty thousand people walked along the funeral route, and national and international figures joined the list of mourners. Pallbearers carried Chavez's simple pine coffin in a procession that ended at Forty Acres. The funeral mass was led by Cardinal Roger M. Mahoney. Author and playwright Luis Valdez said, "Cesar, we have come to plant your heart like a seed. . . . The farm workers shall harvest in the seed of your memory."[15] President Bill Clinton stated, "The labor movement and all Americans have lost a great leader . . . an authentic hero to millions of people throughout the world."[16] Pope John Paul II telegraphed his condolences. The following year, President Clinton posthumously awarded Chavez the Presidential Medal of Freedom; his wife, Helen, accepted the award on his behalf. In addition, Governor Pete Wilson designated March 31 a California state holiday in honor of Cesar Chavez.

Since Chavez's death, some of the victories achieved by the UFW have eroded. But his commitment to nonviolence and legacy of public service made a lasting impact on both American agriculture and the civil rights movement. Chavez became a figure of pride and empowerment for the Chicano community. The movement he created won improvements in pay and living conditions for workers from all backgrounds. But most important, through his acts of sacrifice and dedication, Cesar Chavez became an example of how one person can better the livelihood of many.

NOTES

1. Matt S. Meier and Feliciano Rivera, *The Chicanos: A History of Mexican Americans.* New York: Hill and Wang, 1972, p. 258.

2. Cletus E. Daniel, *Labor Leaders in America*, ed. Melvyn Dubofsky and Warren Van Tine. Chicago: University of Illinois Press, 1987, p. 352.

3. Quoted in Jacques E. Levy, *Cesar Chavez: An Autobiography of La Causa.* New York: Norton, 1975, p. 24.

4. Quoted in Daniel, *Labor Leaders in America*, p. 354.

5. Quoted in Daniel, *Labor Leaders in America*, p. 355.

6. Quoted in Lowrider Magazine Online, "The Roots of Lowriding," www.lowridermagazine.com.

7. Richard Griswold del Castillo and Richard A. Garcia, *Cesar Chavez: A Triumph of Spirit.* Norman: University of Oklahoma Press, 1995, p. 14.

8. Meier and Rivera, *The Chicanos*, p. 257.

9. Del Castillo and Garcia, *Cesar Chavez*, p. 79.

10. Quoted in United Farm Workers, "Farm Workers Remember Rev. Dr. Martin Luther King Jr.," n.d., www.ufw.org.

11. Quoted in United Farm Workers, "The Story of Cesar Chavez," n.d., www.ufw.org.

12. Cesar Chavez, "The New Grape Boycott—Will It Work in the Eighties?" (Harvard Law School Forum speech). www.law.harvard.edu.

13. Quoted in United Farm Workers, "The Story of Cesar Chavez."

14. Del Castillo and Garcia, *Cesar Chavez*, p. 136.

15. Quoted in United Farm Workers, "The Story of Cesar Chavez."

16. White House Office of the Press Secretary, press release, April 23, 1993. www.biblio.org.

Chapter 1

The First
Struggles

**People
Who Made
History**

Cesar Chavez

Early Influences

Jan Young

A pivotal event in the life of Cesar Chavez was the
loss of his family home when Chavez was ten years
old. Over the next few years, the Chavez family faced
corrupt labor contractors, homelessness, and discrimination in their travels as migrant workers. This
article by Jan Young provides insight as to how
through scrimping, creativity, and back-breaking labor the Chavez family was able to deal with the challenges of survival. Jan Young, author of seven books
on American historical figures, chronicles the first
obstacles faced by young Chavez and the resilience
demonstrated by his religious mother and hardworking father.

Cesar Estrada Chavez was born on March 31, 1927, at Yuma,
Arizona, the second oldest child and eldest son of Librado
and Juana Chavez. His paternal grandfather, also named Cesar, had been born in Mexico but had migrated to the United
States during the Mexican Revolution. He became a U.S. cit-
izen and homesteaded 160 acres of land in the Gila River
Valley twenty miles from Yuma. Over the years, as his fifteen
children grew up, some married or drifted away to new
homes, but Librado stayed on helping on the farm and working it for Cesar's grandmother after her husband's death.

Their house was of thick-walled adobe after the style in
Mexico, cool in summer and warm in winter. Though they
were far from wealthy, they managed to live comfortably
with their chickens, livestock, crops of cotton, lettuce, carrots and watermelons and family vegetable garden.

Young Cesar's early years were spent in a warm and lov-
ing family atmosphere surrounded by numerous aunts, un-
cles and cousins. His favorite playmates were his cousin
Manuel, two years older than himself, and his brother
Richard, two years younger. The three boys developed a

Jan Young, *The Migrant Workers and Cesar Chavez*, New York: Julian Messner, 1974.
Copyright © 1974 by Julian Messner. Reproduced by permission.

bond of comradeship that would continue into adulthood.

A devoutly religious woman, Juana Chavez made it part of her faith to help those less fortunate than herself, a philosophy she passed on to her eldest son. During the early years of the depression, the drifting tramps who came through the Gila Valley looking for work were always made welcome at the family's dinner table. But by 1936 the depression had reached out to touch the Chavez family also. There was not enough money to keep up the taxes or pay the water bills, and in 1937, when Cesar was ten years old, the farm was taken away from them. Librado and Juana, with their three sons and two daughters, loaded what possessions they could take with them in their old car and joined the tide of migrant workers who followed the crops from Arizona into Southern California, then up the length of the Central Valley and back south again. In those next years, until he finally dropped out of school after completing the seventh grade, Cesar Chavez estimated that he attended more than thirty different schools.

FOLLOWING THE CROPS

All the years that the Chavez family spent following the crops were difficult, but the first years were the worst. They were naïve and unbelievably innocent of what it took to survive as migrant workers. That first year they signed up with a labor contractor to harvest wine grapes near Fresno in a vineyard with such a scanty crop that all other workers had refused to work on it. For a week the entire family worked alone in the field, and then Mr. Chavez asked for their pay. The contractor explained that it was not his custom to pay until the harvest was finished, but when he learned that they were without money for food he grudgingly loaned them twenty dollars. The Chavezes continued working, making do on the twenty dollars, until the grapes were all picked. But when they went to the contractor's house to collect their back pay, they found that he had gone, taking their money with him.

The following year, in 1938, they ran into another contractor who assured them that they could make a lot of money in the cotton fields at Mendota, east of Fresno. Having grown cotton back in Arizona, they took off eagerly. It was November when they reached Mendota, and the winter rains had begun. There was work only on the rare sunny days between storms. Disgusted with the continual rain and lack of work, the other migrants at the camp began moving out and heading south. The Chavezes did not have the money to leave, so they stayed on even after the electricity was turned off and they were the only family left. To survive, they picked wild greens in the fields and caught fish from the canals. At last relatives in Arizona sent them enough money to get them to Los Angeles, where Mrs. Chavez sold hand crocheting on the streets to make enough for the gas to take them on to Brawley in the Imperial Valley, where winter work was available.

After sleeping in their car for several days they found a house to rent, and for the next couple of years Brawley became their home base. There was not enough work there to support them year round, so each spring they started the long trek from the Imperial Valley up the Central Valley as far as Marysville, picking peas, lettuce, tomatoes, figs, prunes, grapes and apricots, and then, in late November, headed south praying their old car would make it back to Brawley again.

One winter they did not make it. Stranded in Oxnard on the coast, they lived that winter in a tent while Mr. and Mrs. Chavez tried to support them by picking peas. Cesar and Richard collected discarded cigarette packages along the highway, carefully removing the tinfoil inside and saving it in a huge ball. When the ball weighed eighteen pounds, they sold it to a junk dealer for enough money to buy two sweatshirts and a pair of tennis shoes.

A BRUTAL EDUCATION

As they continued working the crops, the family began to learn the tricks of survival. When there was no housing available or they could not afford it, they learned to camp under bridges, which afforded shelter from both the hot summer sun and winter rains. They learned the rotation of the various crops so they could arrive at exactly the right time for each and find work at peak pay. They passed the information that they gleaned on to others to help them avoid the pitfalls into which they themselves had innocently fallen during those first years.

They also learned about discrimination. Back in the Gila River Valley, they had never been aware of any difference between themselves and the Anglo-American farmers, but in California it was different. In most of the schools that Cesar and Richard attended, they were shunted into special class-rooms or annexes just for Mexican children. In Brawley the Mexican-Americans had their own side of town and were not encouraged to go into the Anglo section. To make extra money, Cesar and Richard fixed up a shoe-shine kit and hus-tled business on the streets. Located on the dividing line be-tween the Mexican and Anglo sections of town was a restau-rant which claimed to sell the best hamburgers in the valley. One afternoon, flush with the profits from their shoe-shine business and unaware of the meaning of a sign in the win-dow that said WHITES ONLY, the boys popped into the diner and ordered two hamburgers. "What's matter, you dumb Mex—can't you read?" the waitress said as she ordered them out. Richard was furious, but Cesar, who had ordered the hamburgers, was close to tears with embarrassment. After that it did not take them long to learn that, though they were third generation Americans, because their ancestors had come from Mexico they were second-class citizens.

In 1939, while the family was staying near San Jose, a union tried to organize the workers in the dried-fruit indus-try. Though Librado was never active in union organization, he took out a union card and walked on the picket lines. The strike was quickly broken, but the meetings in the homes and the talk of the men, who hoped briefly that the union would help, made a lasting impression on the twelve-year-old Cesar.

Life in the Labor Camps

Jean Maddern Pitrone

The Chavez family, along with thousands of others in Depression era California, traveled hundreds of miles following harvests throughout the state. This type of labor employed every member of the family, which resulted in fractured formal educations for many migrant worker children, including Cesar and his siblings. Work conditions frequently amounted to indentured servitude; families lived in cramped barracks and crop-picking wages often provided just enough to pay rent. In this selection, excerpted from Jean Maddern Pitrone's 1971 book *Chavez: Man of the Migrants*, Chavez gets his first taste of union action. Jean Maddern Pitrone is the author of ten biographies.

The Chavez family's work treks covered hundreds of miles, reaching a northern point of some 50 miles above Sacramento in California's Central Valley and stretching back through the Santa Clara area, Salinas Valley, San Joaquin Valley, and, in November, to the southernmost Imperial Valley. During the short winter gap, they lived, for a time, in a little rented house in the Mexican-Negro-Japanese-Chinese and migrant-white section of the town of Brawley, where local police watched to see that no intruder ventured into Brawley's better section, known as Anglo-Town.

In Brawley, life for the Chavez family was a continuing struggle to get enough work—any kind of work—to pay the rent and buy food. When there was no money for food, the children gathered mustard greens from ditches for their mother to cook, did odd jobs, and shined shoes at a box they set up at the edge of Anglo-Town. Cesar and his brothers and sisters attended the school for the children of their section of town and quickly learned to work with the broken pencils and ragged books discarded from the Anglo school.

The youthful Cesar soon learned, too, to control his tears (while his more explosive brother Richard found it hard to control his rage) as, during the family's first year of travels, he saw signs on eating places reading NO DOGS OR MEXI-CANS. Refused service in restaurants catering to "White Trade Only" and turned away from restroom facilities in many main-highway gas stations, Librado Chavez began avoiding such unpleasantries by traveling, whenever possible, on bumpy, dusty sideroads. On these sideroads the family could get service at a variety of weatherbeaten shacklike stores, gas stations or eating places in Mexican settlements where the sight of an oil-burning, overloaded car with dark-eyed children packed in among assorted household gear would not offend the established residents of prospering towns or the wealthy tourists of such resorts as Palm Springs.

Hope had died slowly within the Chavez family as, in the early spring of 1938, they had moved north again, up into the southern San Joaquin peach bowl area where hundreds of workers were being hired in the orchards and packing sheds for the peak season ahead. Papa and Mama Chavez and the children settled into labor camp quarters—long bleak barracks concealed behind the packing sheds which were, in turn, fronted by neat administration buildings and attractive staff bungalows bordered with flowers. The fuzz-skinned peaches had to be picked and carefully placed in the small basket hanging from the picker's arm, then as carefully transferred into a larger basket, so that the delicate fruit would not be bruised. In still another camp, the family picked oranges—nipping the stems with clippers and handling the fruit with gloved hands.

The Chavez children soon lost count of the camps in which they had lived as they moved from one to another—over-charged for rental of housing in the labor camps, overcharged for groceries, kerosene and other essentials at the stores located on or near the campgrounds, paid the lowest of wages for the most backbreaking of work under the hot sun, and taken advantage of by mechanics in roadside repair shops as, like the other migrants in their second hand cars and decrepit trucks, they followed the crops, the seasons, the sun, and reports of "higher wages" and "good housing." Invariably, their hopes were destroyed as the next labor camp proved to be little better—sometimes a little worse—than the last.

A MATTER OF SURVIVAL

The small amount of money the Chavez family was able to save from their combined efforts in any single camp was spent, quickly, for any one of a number of emergencies that arose—a replacement of tires or a new battery for the car, shoes for five rapidly growing children, a visit to a doctor's office (where, usually, the doctor was too busy to examine a migrant) or to a hospital emergency room with an ailing child. . . . And then there was the winter's stay in the Imperial Valley when field work was scarce and any earnings quickly were used for food and shelter.

As the family saw the destruction of its hopes, they developed a distrust of the businessmen, casual strangers and crew leaders who encouraged migrants to go to a certain area where work was "plentiful." If it was true that work was plentiful, the workers, purposely recruited in far larger numbers than needed, were even more plentiful, so that workers easily were replaced with others willing to work more cheaply.

Even the Chavez children realized, now, as they picked firm ripe tomatoes from among those already rotting on the vines, that their work in the fields was not helping their parents to accumulate savings for the purchase of a new homesite—that, instead, their daily field work was a matter of food on the table for that night's supper and a matter of day-to-day existence. Although state laws restricted under-age children from working in the fields and specified that school-age children must attend school, the laws were not enforced with any regularity. The children's help was necessary for the family, collectively, to make a living wage, and so parents, growers and truant officers were part of the silent conspiracy to keep the children in the fields. For Cesar, the only relief from the glare of the sun and from the buzzing of gnats around the spoiled tomatoes was the memory of the earlier years when the family had lived in its own home and worked its own fields.

While the juice from the tomatoes soaked his sweat-stained trousers, he thought of the great tree at the side of his grandfather's hacienda and how he and his brother would climb high into the branches and survey the house, the garden and the fields beyond. It was not unusual for the boys to find their mother ladling out extra platefuls of beans from the large pot simmering on the stove when the children came into the house for a meal. Passersby always were made welcome in the Chavez household, and many of these passersby were unemployed men and their families headed westward in search of work in the depression's early years. It was not until Cesar's family had become migrants that the boy realized that his mother's share-with-those-in-need philosophy was not that of most people—certainly not of the crew leaders who tried to cheat workers of their small earnings nor of the farm owners who were unwilling to pay a fair wage to the laborers and who charged them rent for smelly shacks that often had no electricity nor plumbing.

UNION MOVEMENT STIRS HOPE

Cesar was twelve years old and working with his family, picking prunes in the Santa Clara Valley, when the Chavez family was excited by the possibility of taking action to improve working conditions. Here in the Santa Clara area where thousands of workers were needed to pick prunes on some 70,000 acres of orchards, and to pick apricots on another 20,000 acres for the largest dried-fruit packing center in the world, an Anglo stranger had come into the prune-pickers' housing compound to talk to the individual families as they ate their beans and tortillas after their day's work in the fields. Both Cesar and Richard listened as the Anglo explained the CIO's goals to their father, whose dark eyes gleamed with anticipation while the organizer explained that the workers should unite to join the union movement and to strike. Then the growers would be forced to pay higher wages to get their crops picked, the family was told, before the fruit rotted on the trees. For a time—a very short time—even the boys sensed that there was a new vitality in their father's walk and in his voice as he talked some of the other workers into signing union pledges. The strikers were jubilant as, on the first day of their strike, the prunes remained unpicked . . . cautious on the second day as more workers were brought in to replace the strikers, and, admittedly, defeated as, within a few days, the orchards were filled with new recruits and with men who had defected from the picket lines. As the strike petered out to a raggle-taggle ending, the unemployed prune pickers took to the highways again as they moved on to seek work elsewhere.

In the following several years, Librado Chavez joined every union that recruited members from among migrant farm workers, even though each union was soon destroyed by the powerful growers and by the timidity of workers, fearful of losing their jobs—no matter how poorly paid the jobs were. For the Chavez family, the lowest-paid work was a melon-thinning job down in the Imperial Valley where they were paid twelve and a half cents an hour in 1941. Cesar was fourteen years old, now, had attended thirty-seven schools to an eighth grade level, and, after leaving the Imperial Valley in the early spring, was never to return to school.

Chavez Challenges the Status Quo

Ronald B. Taylor

Young Cesar Chavez faced discrimination in many forms as the family followed harvests throughout the state. From frustrated field workers Chavez first learned the tactic of collectively withholding labor. When he moved with his family to Delano, California, he participated in his first disputes with figures of authority. He also tested the practice of movie theater segregation, an action that landed him in jail. A larger problem, which would continue to be faced by the workers for many years, was the Federal recruitment of Mexican laborers in the 1930s, known as the Bracero Program, which supplemented the existing pool of migrant workers and created a large population of inexpensive labor. Journalist Ronald B. Taylor chronicled the travails of the farmworkers and wrote a book about the struggle entitled *Chavez and the Farm Workers*, a selection from which is excerpted here.

As the Chavez family moved through the harvests, ranging as far north as the Sacramento Valley and as far south as the Imperial Valley, they learned their only weapon was their ability to quit, to withhold their labor. Like most migrants, they participated in scores of small strikes. The workers—either as individual families or as an entire crew—would ask for higher wages. If they were rejected they would quit in anger, stalking off the job. . . .

Mrs. Chavez tried to keep her children in school as much as possible. By the time Chavez had dropped out in the 8th grade he had attended so many schools he can never give an accurate count. Sometimes he recalls 30, sometimes 40; the number varies with the telling as Chavez relates his educational background. The classrooms looked the same; the teachers seldom took notice of the migrant children passing through.

Chavez said, "I think that was the worst, not being noticed. The schools treated you like you didn't exist. Their indifference was incredible. When you went into school for the first time the principal and a teacher would discuss where they should put you, right in front of you. It made you feel like you weren't important.

"Then they wouldn't let you talk Spanish. In P.E. they would make you run laps around the track if they caught you speaking Spanish or a teacher in a classroom would make you write 'I won't speak Spanish' on the board 300 times, or I remember once a teacher hung a sign on you that said 'I am a clown, I speak Spanish.'"

In the fall of 1943 the Chavez family moved into the Fresno County raisin harvest, near Biola. The pay was a nickel a tray for cutting and spreading the grapes on paper trays to dry in the 100-degree September sun. Richard and Cesar, working as a team, would start in the vines at dawn. They would work at top speed until 8:30 A.M., when they would stop for a little breakfast, then back again, working as hard as they could until early afternoon, when the heat became so fierce the thick, loose earth burned their feet. By early afternoon they could make 200 to 250 trays each, and they were proud of the $20 to $25 a day they contributed to the family income.

CHAVEZ'S FIRST PROTESTS

The Chavez family returned to Delano that winter, and established a home there. He said, "We had a house on Ellington and 8th Street. There was no development there then, to speak of, and the town itself had maybe 2,500 people. It was a wide-open town with a red-light district with maybe 20 houses. . . ."

He said the whorehouses attracted the servicemen and truck drivers off Highway 99. The truckers used to park their big rigs in front of the Chavez's driveway while they went across the street to get a quick bounce in a squeaky bed. When the truckers ignored the family's protests, Cesar went to the Mexican Society—a group of older men who had been in the Mexican revolution—and asked them to do something.

The old revolutionaries told Cesar to go home, that he was

too young to do anything, and besides, the whorehouses were legal, they were a part of the government in Delano. Young Chavez didn't like the answer, but he could think of nothing else to do. A few nights later he went to the movies in a downtown theater. The audience was segregated. The Anglos sat on one side of the main aisle, the Mexicans on the other.

"I really hadn't thought much about what I was going to do but I had to do something. We were supposed to sit on the south side. I moved over to the north side, but this usherette wouldn't let me sit down.

"I told her, 'Don't touch me, I got a ticket,' and I sat down. She called the assistant manager and he came down. He was hostile and he told to get up, or he would break my arms. When I didn't move he called the manager and he raised hell. It was dark inside and all these people were turning around, looking to see what was happening."

Finally the police were called. They came in, and when Chavez refused to move, they pried his hands loose from the armrests and dragged him out. They took him to the police station. Cesar's friends in the theater called his father. The police kept young Chavez for about an hour, then warned him not to cause any more trouble and turned him back over to his father. Angered and frightened by the confrontation, he wanted to take some kind of legal action, but he did not know how. He knew no lawyers. The incident was put aside, but not forgotten.

The humiliation, anger, and frustration of being powerless made deep impressions on Chavez. He was and still is *Mexican* in the California-migrant-farm worker sense of the word; this Mexican-ness was the only thing he knew from the time the family was displaced from their Arizona farm until he joined the Navy, in 1944. When Cesar reported for basic training in San Diego he had just turned 17, and had never been away from his family; for him the prejudices were clear cut, brown vs. white, but in boot camp in San Diego, he discovered prejudices had other dimensions.

"I saw this white kid fighting, because someone had called him Pollock and I found out he was Polish and he hated that word Pollock. He fought every time he heard it. I began to learn something, that others suffered, too," Chavez said.

Chavez served in the South Pacific, at the tag end of World War II. As a coxswain's apprentice he worked on the small boats, ferrying ship's pilots in and out of the harbor. He recalled, "Once or twice we picked up fliers who went down in the water." He was transferred to Guam, where he worked on the beach, in a paint shop; he was taking tests for a third-class painter's rating when he was discharged in 1946.

After his discharge he hitchhiked to Delano. . . .

THE *BRACERO* PROBLEM

Each spring and summer there were more and more workers in the orchards, vineyards, and fields; where 10 families could work all day finishing out a block of peaches, there would be 20 to 30 families and the work would be completed by noon. Sometimes, when they pulled up to a farm, they were told there was no work at all, but out in the field they would see large crews of single men—*Braceros.*

The *Braceros*—the word means "arm" or strong arm— were Mexican-national contract workers, imported under special treaty with Mexico, to work for specific periods in specific "labor-short" crops. The *Braceros,* first used during the World War II labor-short years, were becoming the "ideal" farm labor force; they replaced the troublesome "Okies" who were off in the defense plants building bombers or tanks. These rural Mexican men, coming from the poorest of circumstances, living in farmer-operated camps, dependent upon farmers for food and transportation, were totally subservient. They could not rebel, and when the work was over they were shipped back to Mexico. Any *Bracero* who protested working or living conditions had his contract terminated and he was swiftly repatriated.

The farmers in Texas and California liked the *Bracero* program so much that by 1945 they were ordering 50,000 contract workers. Ten years later the number had reached 300,000 *Braceros* a year, and this number did not include the *illegal* aliens who were flooding into the farm labor market. As the farmers recruited the *Braceros,* they also attracted tens of thousands of impoverished Mexicans from the villages all over rural Mexico. Those who could not get on the *Bracero* lists paid smugglers to help them slip through the border. In 1945 the U.S. Border Patrol captured 69,000 illegal aliens in the United States; as the demand for *Braceros* rose, the numbers of illegal aliens also rose; by 1953 the farmers were importing 200,000 *Braceros* into the farming states, and the Border Patrol was capturing 800,000 illegal aliens, most of them farm workers.

Numerically the *Braceros* were never more than a minority of the total work force; in California and Texas at the peak of the harvest season, one worker in three was a contract Mexican national, but this statistic did not measure the impact the program had on farm labor. *Braceros* dominated some crops, like tomatoes. The local tomato pickers then had to seek work in other crops, like grapes, where there were already enough workers. With more than enough workers the grape farmer had no reason to increase his pay scale. The key to the vicious cycle lay in the farmers' ability to set "prevailing wages" so low local workers would not work the crop; this produced the "labor shortage" needed to certify the crop for *Braceros*, and it produced a surplus of workers in other crops that had a chilling effect on the total farm wage structure.

The effect of this could plainly be seen in the San Joaquin Valley. Along the west side of the valley and down into Kern County the large row-crop farms used most of the Mexican aliens, and during the late 1940s the prevailing wage on the west side was 80 to 85 cents an hour. The state average at the time was a dollar, and many of the small family farms along the east side of the valley were offering "a dollar and a dime" to attract workers away from the corporate farms. As the cost of living went up and farm wages remained the same, or sagged, the local workers became angry and rebellious.

In the fall of 1947—as the Chavez family moved into the Delano grape harvest—the DiGiorgio Fruit Corporation workers near Arvin went out on strike. The news spread quickly: 1,100 workers on this big ranch had asked for a 10-cents-an-hour pay hike, for grievance procedures, for a seniority system, and for recognition of their union, the National Farm Labor Union. The NFLU was an affiliate of the American Federation of Labor, and from the outset other members of the federation began to support the farm workers' strike with money, clothing, and food. Urban churchmen and liberals took up the workers' cause, volunteering time, money, and supplies. . . .

In the fall of 1949 the San Joaquin Valley Agriculture Labor Bureau set the cotton-picking rate at $2.50 a hundred, down 50 cents from the previous season. The NFLU capitalized on the anger this move generated among the cotton pickers, calling a general cotton strike throughout the San Joaquin Valley. The workers—many of them veterans of

1933—responded, and strike camps were set up throughout the valley. It was in this strike that Cesar Chavez got his first taste of a major farm labor strike. . . .

The strike lasted a little more than two weeks. Then, with the help of the state mediation service, the NFLU succeeded in getting the Agriculture Labor Bureau to reverse its decision. The picking rate was set back at $3 a hundred pounds. The cotton pickers went back to work. Chavez drove back to Delano, to join his family in the grape harvest. But the whole experience had been unsatisfactory, unsettling. The strikes, the picket lines and caravans, the meetings in the afternoons, all had whetted his appetite, but it had been so disorganized. He wanted to learn how to avoid the mistakes he felt the NFLU had made, but there was no one to help him.

A Commitment to Persevere

Peter Matthiessen

While he was living in the San Jose barrio of *Sal Si Puedes* in the 1950s, Chavez met Fred Ross, an activist who would play a key role in the development of Chavez's career. Ross eventually recruited Chavez into the Community Service Organization founded by radical activist Saul Alinsky. The CSO strived to empower traditionally oppressed workers through voter registration drives and community organizing.

Peter Matthiessen served as New York State Writers Institute State Author from 1995 to 1997 and was elected to the American Academy of Arts and Letters in 1974. He is also a prolific novelist and cofounder of *The Paris Review*. In the following selection based on personal interviews, Matthiessen traces Chavez's steps from his induction into formal community service to the creation of a union of his own design.

In the days that followed, I was able to piece together the story of how Chavez became an organizer. Chavez, who described most of it himself, picketed the cotton fields at Corcoran for the National Agricultural Workers Union in 1946, when he was nineteen, and watched the union fail. Subsequently he would mutter about the frustrations of the poor to his wife, Helen, and his brother Richard, but he saw no way to put his outrage into action until 1952. That year he and Richard lived across the street from each other in San Jose, and worked together in the apricot groves. The Los Angeles headquarters of Saul Alinsky's Community Service Organization wanted to set up a chapter there, and among the names given to the CSO organizer by the parish priest, Father Donald McDonnell, was that of Cesar Chavez.

"I came home from work and this gringo wanted to see

me. In those days when a gringo wanted to see you, it was something special; we never heard anything from whites unless it was the police. So anyway, Helen says, 'Oh no, it must be something good for Mexicans—money and a better job and things!'" Chavez's expression conveyed what he had thought about promises of something good for Mexicans. "You see, Stanford University had people nosing around, writing all kinds of screwy reports about how Mexicans eat and sleep, you know, and a lot of dirty kind of stuff, and Berkeley had its guys down there, and San Jose State—all the private colleges; they were interested in the worst *barrio*, the toughest slum, and they all picked Sal Si Puedes."

"What?"

"Sal—"

"'Escape If You Can'?"

"Yah. That's what that *barrio* was called, because it was every man for himself, and not too many could get out of it, except to prison. . . .

"So he came and talked to me. I was very closed, I didn't say a thing. I just let him talk. I'd say 'Yes' and nod my head, but half the time I was plotting how to get him. Still, there were certain things that struck me. One of them was how much I didn't like him even though he was sincere. I couldn't admit how sincere he was, and I was bothered by not being able to look at it. And the other thing was, he wore kind of rumpled clothes, and his car was very poor. And his flawless pronunciation of the Mexican language—that *really* impressed me. It's minor, I know, but I was impressed. . . .

He talked about the CSO and then the famous Bloody Christmas case a few years before, when some drunken cops beat up some Mexican prisoners down in L.A. I didn't know what the CSO was or who this guy Fred Ross [CSO organizer and Chavez's visitor] was, but I knew about the Bloody Christmas case, and so did everybody in that room; some cops had actually been sent to jail for brutality, and it turned out that this miracle was thanks to the CSO. . . .

"Anyway, I walked out with him to his car and thanked him for coming, and then I kind of wanted to know—well, what next? He said, 'Well, I have another meeting, and I don't suppose you'd like to come?' I said, 'Oh yes, I would.' I told the others I'd be right back, and I got in his car and went with him, and that was it.

"That first meeting . . . I'd never been in a group before,

and I didn't know a thing. Somebody asked for a motion, and I didn't know what the hell they were talking about. I tried to get answers from my friends, and none of us knew. We were just a bunch of *pachucos*—you know, long hair and pegged pants. But Fred wanted to get the *pachucos* involved—no one had really done this—and he knew how to handle the difficulties that came up, and he didn't take for granted a lot of little things that other people take for granted when they're working with the poor. He had learned, you know. Finally I said, 'What about the farm workers?' and he said that the CSO could be a base for organizing farm workers, and it was a good prediction, not exactly as he envisioned it, but it came about.". . .

THE CSO YEARS

Chavez first joined the CSO as a volunteer in a voter-registration drive: the organization of Mexican-American bloc voting was the first lesson in his understanding of a power base. "Most of the volunteers were college people, or had good jobs—very few were farm workers. I had a part-time job in a lumberyard. Voter registration depended on as many evenings as you could give, and soon so many people stopped showing up that we had to find a new chairman every day. Finally I was the only one who went with Fred every night, so he made me chairman. . . .

A few months later, at Fred Ross's recommendation, Chavez was hired by Saul Alinsky as a staff member, at $35 a week. After six months in San Jose, he took over Ross's CSO chapter in nearby Decoto, and two months after that, he was asked to start a new chapter in Oakland. He was still so poorly educated that he could scarcely read; he was small and thin and looked much younger than his twenty-five years, and he lived in terror of his own house meetings. He would drive back and forth in front of the house where a meeting was to be held, then dart in and sit in the corner until forced to identify himself as the organizer. But his first big meeting in Oakland was a turning point, and Fred recognized it; in 1953 he put Chavez in charge of the whole San Joaquin Valley.

In the next few years Chavez established chapters in Madera, Bakersfield, and many other towns. He was already a good organizer, and he got better as he developed techniques of his own. He learned to beware of established precepts, to cut around the entrenched local leadership, to avoid philosophizing in favor of clear illustration and example ("You have to draw a simple picture and color it in," he says), and above all, he recognized that organizing requires time. He estimates that 40 to 50 percent of the farm workers are illiterate in English and nearly so in Spanish. "You have to spend time with people, that's all. If a man's interested, it makes no difference if he can read or write; he is a man."

In the early fifties the Cold War wave of reaction that congealed around McCarthyism was prospering in the Valley, which since the thirties had been hypersensitive to anything radical or "Red," and a man who encouraged Mexican-Americans to vote was an obvious subversive. Cowed by local patriots, his own people in the Madera chapter began investigating Chavez for symptoms of the dread Communism, then backed off, abashed, when he challenged them to do so in his presence, not behind his back. The experience taught him the great folly of expecting gratitude, and more important, how pathetically afraid poor people were. Subsequently he had to return to San Jose and rebuild the CSO chapter: in the absence of strong leadership, the people had retreated into their apathy.

Nevertheless, the CSO was gaining strength, and its new power was reflected in the increased expense accounts of its staff. Politicians and professional people attached themselves to the organization for prestige purposes, and meanwhile the leadership was opposing Chavez's impractical demand that they try to organize a union of farm workers. At meeting after meeting Chavez spoke out against the new luxurious habits and the softening of purpose, the "erosion" that he speaks of to this day as the thing most to be feared in his own union; to symbolize his protest, he showed up at meetings unshaven and tieless—he has been tieless ever since—and refused any further increase in his own salary. "That salary was almost an insult," he remarked, still cross about it, and I asked him why. "Well, there were certain rules I set myself as an organizer," he said, "and I had to obey them. To come in a new car to organize a community of poor people—that doesn't work. And if you have money but dress like they do, then it's phony. Professional hunger." He grunted in disgust. "You can be hungry and have money in the bank, or you can be hungry and have nowhere to go. There's a big difference.". . .

TASTING DEFEAT

For a year and a half, between August 1958 and November 1959, Chavez had organized the farm workers of Oxnard against the inequities of the *bracero* program, which was being abused for the growers' benefit by both the Farm Placement Service of the California Department of Employment and the Bureau of Employment Security of the U.S. Department of Labor. Work cards issued to domestic laborers by the FPS proved useless when any *braceros* were available—according to Public Law 78, the reverse should have been true—and Chavez, knowing that pleas for justice would be useless, documented hundreds of cases of illegal job discrimination by taking groups of jobless workers to fill out work cards, day after day, and keeping a record of the results. Then he staged field sit-ins—his men went out and stationed themselves opposite the *braceros* who had taken their jobs—and a protest march, at the end of which the cards were burned in a gesture of contempt for the corruption of the hiring program. The press was invited to the fire.

All of these maneuvers anticipated tactics that Chavez would refine in his own union, and they worked; in the glare of publicity, the domestic workers returned to work. They were eighteen hundred strong, and loyal to Chavez, and they held firm when he demanded better wages and conditions. The growers met his terms, though not officially; concealing their names, they would call up and say "please send me the workers. I'll be waiting by the church in a yellow pickup." "This is when I really learned," Chavez says, "that the growers weren't invincible." He now feels that he could have got a union shop, but his CSO job did not permit him to negotiate a contract. For fifteen months he had worked twenty hours a day, his weight had shrunk to one hundred and twenty-nine pounds, and he watched in despair as the Packinghouse union of the AFL-CIO took over what was, potentially, the first effective farm workers union in California. Under mechanical trade-union direction, an organization which had been built on dedication soon disintegrated.

According to Manuel Chavez, his cousin offered a year's service without salary to the CSO if the organization would support a new union of farm workers. At a CSO convention in Calexico, in March 1962, the board voted down Chavez's plan for the last time, and Chavez rose and said simply, "I resign." People immediately jumped to their feet and started arguing with one another, as if Chavez weren't there. He couldn't resign, they decided. But he had, and he and Dolores Huerta and Fred Ross went across the border to Mexicali to get something to eat. They were all very depressed. Chavez told me later that he had been "heartbroken"; he had known that he would have to quit, but it was the CSO that had changed his life. . . .

BIRTH OF A UNION

When Chavez left the CSO in 1962, [Dolores Huerta] told him she would be honored to work for him—the verb is hers—and after 1962 she was a lobbyist for his National Farm Workers Association at the state capitol in Sacramento. . . .

"Cesar had studied the structure of the CSO," Mrs. Huerta says, "and he tried to correct its mistakes in NFWA: mainly, he wanted the people who did the work to make the decisions. He wanted the workers to participate, and he still does, because without that, the Union has no real strength. This is why he would never accept outside money, not until the strike began: he wanted the workers to see that they could pay for their own union." Very early in his struggle, Chavez turned down a private grant of $50,000 that was offered without conditions; he felt that the gift would put pressure on him to obtain immediate results. "Manuel and I almost quit," Richard Chavez says.

In his first hard year, when his own $1,200 savings were all spent, Chavez became so desperate that he had to go to people to beg food, like a monk seeking alms. This was hard on his pride, as he admits, but he sees it as a blessing. "Then and later," he has said, "we got some of our best members by asking for food. The people who give you their food give you their hearts."

Chavez got up early every morning and worked until midnight, taking a survey up and down the Valley to find out what farm workers really wanted. With his son Birdie (Anthony), who was then four, he went from door to door and out into the fields, distributing eighty thousand cards that asked the workers how much they thought they should be earning. At that time the average wage was 90 cents an hour, and it is a measure of their despair that most of the workers said that what they deserved was $1.10 or perhaps $1.25. Occasionally a man would say that he deserved $1.50 or even $1.75, or he might scrawl a note of encouragement or hope on his card. These people Chavez visited in person, and many became the first members of his association. . . .

The early members of the Union were people of exceptional faith, and one of the first was a man named Manuel Rivera. He had come to Chavez in 1963 with the complaint that his labor contractor not only refused to tell him what his hourly wage was for work he had already done, but had kicked him out of the truck when he protested this and let him walk back to town. The police had shown no interest in his case. Chavez learned that Rivera's old car had broken down for good, and that after three days in Delano, the Rivera family was still waiting at the bus station. The Chavezes took the whole family into their own small house, and lent Rivera the now defunct Volvo that sits outside the Chavez house; later, he found them a place to stay, and when Rivera had saved a little money, a cheap car.

When Rivera asked how much he owed him, Chavez answered that he didn't owe him anything; he owed help to other farm workers. Rivera returned Chavez's old car, all polished up; then he disappeared and Chavez forgot him. But six months later he showed up again. Over Chavez's protest, Rivera paid union dues for all the months since Chavez had taken him in, and on the job he spoke so fervently of Chavez that he brought in over one hundred new members. "That spirit was what we were looking for," Chavez says, "and it is our strength."

The Strike

Andrew Kopkind

On September 16, 1965, Mexican Independence day,
Chavez and his fledgling union voted to join a labor
strike in the vineyards of Delano, California, initiated
by activist Larry Itilong's Agricultural Workers Organizing Committee. This action became known as the
Great Grape Strike. In January 1966 Andrew Kopkind reported on the Delano strike and remarked on
the challenges unique to this particular struggle. He
noted that Chavez hoped to create a union which
would expand upon the immediate goals of pay eq-
uity and worker safety, with the ultimate goal of improving society at large. Author and journalist Andrew Kopkind traveled the world and wrote about
radical politics for *The Nation* and *The Village Voice.*
In this selection Kopkind chronicles the moment
when strikers first hit the fields and the subsequent
local and national response.

The great central valleys of California have produced almost
as much literature as fruits and vegetables: Mark Twain,
Frank Norris, [John] Steinbeck, [William] Saroyan and a
hundred off-shoots grew amidst the beets and grapes and
cotton and spinach. From it emerges a rough provincial
epic: the struggle of poor settlers against an uncompromising land and the equally uncompromising businesses and
bosses who exploit them.

The epic hero of these times is Cesar Chavez, a short, dark,
mild Mexican-American who is building a strike of grape-
pickers in the San Joaquin Valley into a new kind of labor
war. It is a long time since the valley saw such battles; Chavez
says the strike is the biggest organizing effort in California
agriculture since the Modesto "cotton wars" of the late 'thirties. Whether Chavez will succeed where everyone else failed
is still problematic. The strike is in its fifth month, and the

Andrew Kopkind, "The Grape Pickers' Strike," *The New Republic,* January 29, 1966,
pp. 12–15. Copyright © 1966 by The New Republic, Inc. Reproduced by permission.

grape harvest on the 35 ranches affected was more bountiful, if less profitable, than ever before. But Chavez's idea is not primarily to win small benefits or even long contracts. He is out to develop a community of farm workers, and his methods are more like a civil rights worker's in Mississippi or a ghetto organizer's in Chicago than a union leader's. He is not in the valley for a season of agitating. He came to stay.

EARLY STRIKE ATTEMPTS

Chavez was born in Arizona. His family came to California during the depression, and he grew up in the valley town of Delano, now the epicenter of the 400-square-mile strike zone. For a time he worked among Mexican-Americans on the staff of Saul Alinsky's Community Service Organization. Three years ago he and two other workers left CSO to form the independent National Farm Workers Association. Wages and working conditions were the obvious first concerns of organizing: farm workers in Delano, for instance, have a median family income of about $2,000 a year—and often 10 children to support (the California median is $6,726). State standards (toilets and drinking water in the fields, rest periods) for farm work are largely ignored. Worst of all, the workers have no right to organize, no guarantee of a minimum wage and no protection under federal labor laws.

Chavez tried small strikes against individual growers up and down the valley, but his principal effort was in Delano, where he had lived and worked, and where his wife was raised. Last spring he applied for a Poverty Program grant to train community organizers in money management, literacy teaching, family education—the skills required to bring the grape-pickers in from the fringes of life in their own town.

The proposal was going through the Washington maze when, on September 8, AFL-CIO farm labor organizers called a strike in Delano. Big labor's history of organizing California's "agribusiness" had not been noticeably successful. In 1959, the labor federation formed an Agricultural Workers Organizing Committee (AWOC) and sent an agent up and down the valleys in search of members. The main effort centered in the Imperial Valley of Southern California. A long, bitter strike of lettuce-pickers finally collapsed, in early 1961, when two unions fell into a jurisdictional dispute over the membership of the workers. Labor leadership in Washington let the effort fail.

For the most part, the Mexican-Americans did not trust the "Anglo" labor organizers; they suspected the agents were luring workers into agricultural unions for no better reason than to collect dues and help the industrial unions—which frequently discriminated against the Latins. And so when the AWOC members walked out of the Delano fields, there were few Mexican-Americans among them. Most of the AWOC strikers were Filipinos.

Chavez had thought his community was ill-prepared for a strike, and he was reluctant to risk failure. But in a few days he saw that it would be far worse to break the strike by ignoring it, and his Farm Workers Association formed a joint strike committee with the AFL-CIO leadership. The alliance has held up well, but the character of the strike has been almost completely molded by Chavez. He invited workers of the Congress of Racial Equality and the Student Nonviolent Coordinating Committee [SNCC] into Delano to help organize and to help picket. He adopted a credo of nonviolence, and proclaimed it to the community and the growers (it was, in different ways, irritating to both). He encouraged clergymen to help the strike, and he went to Stanford and Berkeley to get student support. His constituency was developing in the same groups that had been backing the civil rights movement: students, preachers and middle-class liberals. What was amazing was that they had forgotten about labor organizing for 25 years or more, and were now coming back.

STRIKERS HIT THE FIELDS

In two weeks, the growers' work force was reduced by over half. Then the scabs started coming—first from other valley towns, and when they joined the picket lines or refused to work, from out-of-state. Growers bused in workers from Texas and old Mexico. Some hired "wetbacks." The *bracero* program (importation of cheap Mexican labor under federal auspices) had officially ended 10 months earlier, and the resulting shortage of farm workers made a strike seem feasible. But Labor Secretary Willard Wirtz caved in halfway through the season. He allowed the importation of 20,000 Mexicans, and the sudden surplus encouraged the growers to hold out.

Chavez and the AWOC leaders were asking for a minimum wage of $1.40 an hour, and an incentive rate of 25 cents per basket (a good worker picks about four baskets an hour). The average wage in the valley was $1.20 an hour and 10 cents per basket. The strikers also demanded enforcement of the "standard" working conditions. But more than that, they wanted recognition as a union. The growers flatly refused. All but three of the ranchers refused even to open the registered letters Chavez sent asking for negotiations on the eve of the strike. The growers treated the strikers as if they were members of the Viet Cong: ignore them and they will go away.

The strikers did not disappear, and although the imported workers were getting much of the harvest in, the growers felt beleaguered. Teams of roving pickets started at four in the morning and followed work crews. As the day began, the pickets stood at the roadside and shouted *"Huelga!"* ("Strike!") to those in the fields. At first, relatives were shouting to relatives; then most of the Delano workers were in the road shouting to bused-in strikebreakers. The growers went to court and got a temporary restraining order forbidding the pickets to shout, and the growers moved scabs to the middle of fields to avoid contact with the pickets. Some growers went down the margin of their fields with spraying machines, shooting insecticide and fertilizer at the pickets. More commonly, foremen would race along the roadside in tractors, swirling up dust to choke the strikers. Some put farm machinery between the workers and the pickets, or followed the pickets with machine motors racketing at full throttle to drown out their calls. . . .

LOCAL AND NATIONAL RESPONSE

Police and sheriff's deputies were usually on the growers' side. A minister was arrested for reading Jack London's definition of a scab ("a two-legged animal with a corkscrew soul, a water-logged brain, and a combination backbone made of jelly and glue. Where others have hearts, he carries a tumor of rotten principles."). Soon afterward, 44 pickets were arrested. Dolores Huerta, the Farm Workers Association vice president, was arrested twice in a week; the second time, she and a group of strikers were charged with trespassing and released on a total payment of $12,144 in bail. The few growers arrested for violence were let go on their own recognizance. Chavez and a Catholic priest were arrested for "violating air space" of a grower. They had flown in the priest's plane to make contact with pickets sequestered in mid-field. Larry Itliong, the leading Filipino organizer for AWOC, was arrested on very dubious charges of "malicious mischief."

The growers managed to bring in all but about 500 of the 50,000 acres of grapes, but their profits were cut. The unskilled laborers spoiled tons of grapes that the trained Delano workers could have packed carefully. Labor importation costs were huge; distribution was hindered by picket lines around trucks and on the San Francisco docks (Harry Bridges' longshoremen's union refused to load the *President Wilson* with Delano grapes bound for the Orient). Teamsters were, at least theoretically, helpful; the truck drivers were pledged to honor the picket lines, but AWOC strikers claim that truckers merely stepped from their cabs at the lines and let growers' representatives drive them across for loading. But Teamsters cooperated at the produce markets. . . .

The strike itself is continuing through the pruning season. Operations in the vineyards during the winter and spring months call for fewer but more highly skilled workers, and

A CALL FOR SACRIFICE

In a 1966 meeting with clergy sympathetic to the plight of farmworkers, Cesar Chavez outlined his vision for an innovative union. He stressed that the success of this union demanded further sacrifice and significant investment on the part of the workers.

We knew farm workers could be organized and we were going to do it. We weren't going to accept failure. But we were going to make sure that workers contributed to doing this organizing job. That has never been done in the history of this country.

So we began the drive to get workers to pay dues so we could live, so we could just survive. . . . At a farm workers convention, we told them we (the organizers) had nothing to give them except the dream that it might happen. But we couldn't continue unless they were willing to make a sacrifice. At that meeting everyone wanted to pay $5.00 or $8.00 a month. We balked and said, "No, no. Just $3.50. that's all we need." There were about 280 people there, and 212 signed up and paid the $3.50 (equal to more than $10.00 in current dollars) in the first month. . . .

I went to a farm worker's home in McFarland, 7 miles south of Delano. It was. . .winter. And there was no work. I knew it. And everyone knew it. As I knocked on the door, the guy in the little two-room house was going to the store with a $5.00 bill

Chavez and AWOC hope that the strikebreakers will not be able to do it. Consumer boycotts of Delano grapes and wine have spread in California, and civil rights and religious groups are hoping to make them nationwide. (The major producer is Schenley, which makes Cresta Blanca and Roma wines from Delano grapes.) A group of 11 Protestant, Catholic and Jewish clergymen went to Delano last month and issued a strong statement for the strikers: "Those who labor on our California farms deserve the same active support that . . . Christians and Jews have given to the basic demands for justice for Negroes in the South." (The Catholic was criticized by his superiors for the action.) . . .

CHAVEZ'S PROMISING MODEL

Farm labor remains the last unorganized bloc of American workers. No one has any reliable methods yet for organizing the migrant workers, but Chavez's model is at least promising for the laborers already settled in towns. He disdains the

---

to get groceries. And there I was. He owed $7.00 because he was one full month behind plus the current one. So I'd come for $7.00. But all he had was $5.00. I had to make a decision. Should I take $3.50 or shouldn't I? It was very difficult. Up to this time I had been saying, "They should be paying. And if they don't pay they'll never have a union." $3.50 worth of food wasn't really going to change his life one way or the other that much. So I told him, "You have to pay at least $3.50 right now or I'll have to put you out of the union." He gave me the $5.00. We went to the store and changed the $5.00 bill. I got the $3.50 and gave him the $1.50. I stayed with him. He bought $1.50 worth of groceries and went home.

That experience hurt me but it also strengthened my determination. If this man was willing to give me $3.50 on a dream, when we were really taking the money out of his own food, then why shouldn't we be able to have a union—however difficult. There had never been a successful union for farm workers. Every . . . attempt had been defeated. People were killed. They ran into every obstacle you can think of. The whole agricultural industry along with government and business joined forces to break the unions and keep them from organizing. But with the kind of faith this farm worker had why couldn't we have a union?

Cesar Chavez, *Social Policy*, Fall 2001.

traditional method of industrial unionizing:

"The danger is that we will become like the building trades," he said in an interview with the SNCC newspaper, *The Movement.* "Our situation is similar—being the bargaining agent with many separate companies and contractors. We don't want to model ourselves on industrial unions; that would be bad. We want to get involved in politics, in voter registration, not just contract negotiation. Under the industrial union model, the grower would become the organizer. He would enforce the closed shop system; he would check off the union dues. One guy—the business agent—would become king. Then you get favoritism, corruption. The trouble is that no institution can remain fluid. We have to find some cross between being a movement and being a union. The membership must maintain control; the power must not be centered in a few."

Chavez thinks that industrial unions lost their opportunity to keep fluid, to remain progressive, when they concentrated all their efforts on winning a contract—and then quit. His Farm Workers Association is building cooperative institutions—a credit union, co-op stores and gas stations, a funeral insurance club, and services to help Spanish-speaking semiliterates get what's coming to them, from driving licenses to welfare assistance. More than that, he wants to see the grape-pickers of Delano become a powerful part of their community, as their numbers and their economic roles indicate that they should.

Quiet—withdrawn, even—and magnetic, Chavez is often compared to SNCC's Bob Moses, who had the same kind of communitarian vision when he went to Mississippi in 1961. Chavez carries less metaphysical baggage around than Moses did (Chavez is, after all, a generation older), but it is clear that they are both working from the same conception of a good, if not necessarily Great, society. It is far from the individualistic idea the unions had a half century ago. The end of that process was simply to give workers a leg up to the middle class, and be done with them. The new way is quite different—to give workers a decent income and all the while build a society in which they can participate in the decisions which will affect their lives. As it is now, they must leave those decisions to the growers.

CHAPTER 2

THE SOCIAL
AND POLITICAL
IMPACT OF
CHAVEZ'S WORK

CESAR CHAVEZ

Consequences of Civil Disobedience

Mark Day

Father Mark Day, a Roman Catholic priest, worked directly with the United Farm Workers Organizing Committee (UFWOC) during the crucial years of 1967 to 1970. In the following selection, Day describes the jailing of Cesar Chavez for disobeying a court order in regards to a strike against lettuce growers in Salinas, California. The event attracted local and international attention, including visits from prominent political figures and civil rights activists. The impact of Chavez's incarceration rippled through the throngs of Chavez supporters, known as *Chavistas*, and led many to reflect on what it meant to be committed to the movement. In this selection Day focuses on the ruminations of some of those closest to Chavez, who describe both the scene and the fallout. Father Day lives in Vista, California.

"I'm in good spirits, and they're very kind to me. I was spiritually prepared for this confinement; I don't think the judge was unfair. I am prepared to pay the price for civil disobedience. I am still very committed, and I'm not bitter at all.

"At this point in our struggle there is more need than ever to demonstrate our love for those who oppose us. Farm workers are wounded every day by being denied representation of the union of their choice. Jail is a small price to pay to help right that injustice."

> —Statement released by Cesar Chavez from
> the Monterey County jail, December 5, 1970

Salinas was wet, cold, and windy on the morning of December 4, when Cesar was to appear in court before Monterey County Superior Court Justice Gordon Campbell. Chavez was to show cause why he had not obeyed an earlier court order, which demanded that he terminate the boycott against the lettuce-growing company of Bud Antle Produce.

I arrived at the Farm Workers Office on East Alisal Street at 8 A.M. in a drizzling rain. Hundreds of workers were arriving from all over California to join the mass demonstration at the courthouse. I recognized faces from Coachella, Fresno, Fillmore, Delano, Earlimart, Bakersfield, and several other farm towns. A procession was formed, led by the officers of the union: Larry Itliong, Dolores Huerta, Phillip Veracruz, Julio Hernandez, Andy and Luming Imutan, and Gil Padilla. Father Dave Duran asked me to join him near the head of the column, but I decided to drop back and walk with Eloise, one of Cesar's daughters. . . .

The march on the Salinas courthouse coincided with reports that the lettuce boycott was successful, despite grower propaganda to the contrary. In two short months of boycotting, sufficient pressure had been applied to induce Freshpict, the Purex subsidiary, to sign a contract with UFWOC. Shortly after the signing, Freshpict's president, Howard Leach, and its northern California manager, Daryl Arnold, both resigned from their posts, calling the agreement "inflationary and unrealistic." It seems odd to me that these affluent agribusiness executives could have pangs of conscience regarding the modest contract gained by the UFWOC bargaining team.

On the same eventful day, December 4, Pic'N'Pac . . . signed a contract with UFWOC, and Judge Anthony Brazil issued an injunction banning all boycott activities against Bud Antle Produce. The ruling was that Antle had been under contract with Teamsters Local 890 since 1961.

On October 26, the Teamsters, represented by their acting president Frank Fitzsimmons, and president George Meany, of the AFL-CIO, reached an accord that UFWOC would continue to represent field workers, while the Teamsters would have jurisdiction over workers in food-processing plants, warehouses, and markets.

But the question still remained: What was to be done about the two hundred contracts that the Teamsters had hurriedly signed with lettuce and vegetable growers in four California valleys? Teamster organizer William Grami could only say that the contracts were in a state of limbo and that all dues collected from the workers were being held in escrow.

On November 17, Justice Campbell ordered UFWOC to

post a $2.75 million bond in the event that financial damage might accrue to Bud Antle Produce because of the boycott.

THE TRIAL

As Cesar Chavez entered the Monterey County courthouse, he knew that it would be difficult to fight the contempt-of-court charge. Campbell was a longtime friend of some of the Salinas growers, and, as an attorney, had defended the growers in previous labor disputes.

The corridors of the courthouse were jammed with farm workers. A newsman later remarked, "You couldn't hear a sound. You would never know all those people were out there."

Seated in the dock were Cesar Chavez and the attorneys for the defense, Jerry Cohen and William Carder. On the opposite side were two members of the Antle family and their attorneys, Richard B. Maltzman and Philip Bass.

UFWOC's position remained that it was in excess of the court's jurisdiction and unconstitutional to be compelled to obey an order that was under appeal. Bud Antle had refused to negotiate with UFWOC and wanted to continue his "sweetheart" relationship with Teamsters Local 890. UFWOC further asserted that many field workers were never covered by the contract until September, 1970, when Chavez arrived in the valley.

Father Austin Morris, a professor of labor law at the University of San Francisco, had made a study of the Antle contract. "The Teamsters loaned money to Antle in order to bail him out of bankruptcy in the early '60s," Morris told me. "The contract between Antle and the Teamsters was the strangest thing I ever saw. Even though the rest of the growers were furious at Antle for signing it, it was merely a legal formality and literally had no provisions to better the conditions of the workers. To call it a sweetheart contract would be putting it mildly. It seems to me that the contract could have no binding force, either legally or morally, since it was executed with a company-assisted union. The proof of this came when Chavez called the strike. Eighty per cent of Antle's workers walked out on strike, favoring UFWOC. These workers certainly had no allegiance to the Teamsters union."

Since the Dow Chemical Company had purchased 17,000 acres of land from Bud Antle and later leased it back to Antle, a boycott was initiated against Dow. . . .

THE VERDICT

After more than four hours of court proceedings, Campbell found Cesar in contempt of court, fined him $1,000, and sentenced him to jail indefinitely until he "called off the boycott against Bud Antle, Inc., and the Dow Chemical Corporation."

As we left the courtroom, I could see that Helen Chavez, a strong and vivacious woman, was angry. Weeping, Sally Chavez, her sister-in-law, embraced her. A rally was held outside the courthouse and Cesar's request to the farm workers was announced over a bullhorn and before the TV cameras: "Boycott Antle! Boycott Dow! Boycott the Hell Out of Them!"

The farm workers were also angry and shouted *Lo Compraron!* and *Vamos todos a la carcel!* (They bought off the judge! and If Cesar goes to jail, we all go!).

Dolores Huerta and Larry Itliong then spoke to the crowd. Itliong told the workers that this was another example of how the growers can utilize the power of the courts "to keep us poor." But Dolores and Itliong asked for a tough but nonviolent effort against Dow and Antle. "Let us work nonviolently and boycott Dow and Antle from one end of the world to the other," Dolores said.

GROWERS PROTEST KENNEDY VISIT

A few days later, Ethel Kennedy paid a surprise visit to Cesar at the Salinas jail. Ethel, wearing a navy-blue pants suit, was escorted to a candlelight vigil and Mass outside the jail by Jerry Cohen and Rafer Johnson, the athlete, who was acting as her bodyguard. Two thousand workers attended the service. On the opposite side of the street, three hundred "citizens committee" pickets shouted, "Ethel, Go Home" and several other epithets directed against the Kennedy family. Among the opposition were several "prominent" Salinas growers. Their ugly performance, carried by nationwide television, undoubtedly gained more supporters for UFWOC's cause.

"They couldn't have done more for us if they had hired fifty apes," Jerry Cohen told me. "Ethel locked arms with Rafer Johnson and me. We were surrounded by a cordon of sheriff's deputies as we entered the jail. Even with all that protection, some grower tried to hit Ethel or grab her hair. A deputy threw him a karate chop that caused him to recoil in pain. After we had arrived in the visitors' section of the jail, Ethel turned to me and said, 'Gee, you guys throw weird parties!'

With that, the tension broke, and we all laughed hilariously!"

I thought of Senator Robert F. Kennedy's two previous visits to Delano and said to Jerry that the Kennedy wit and presence were always with us when we needed them.

Shortly thereafter, in mid-December, Mrs. Coretta Scott King [widow of Dr. Martin Luther King Jr.] came to the Salinas jail to show her support for Cesar.. . .

THE STATE OF THE MOVEMENT

It was raining in Los Angeles when I visited Sam Kushner, a heavyset, middle-aged man who is the southern California bureau chief of the *People's World* newspaper. . . .

Sam and I talked at length about the strikes in Delano and Salinas. I asked him what he felt was the real significance of the recent victories. "I think that the hiring hall is the best thing that ever happened to farm workers. The fact that a worker still has to work under a labor contractor in many places is one of the most degrading things about agriculture. The hiring hall does away with all the abuses of the labor contractors.

"I will never forget the time I covered the infamous 'shape up' in Calexico. Thousands of farm workers come across the border in the wee hours of the morning from Mexicali in order to find work in the Imperial Valley. Labor contractors choose the most able-bodied workers and load them into trucks and buses. The weak and the aged are left behind.

"On this occasion, I noticed a very young and attractive girl, who appeared to have been left behind. I asked her opinions about the labor contractors and growers. Much to my surprise, she had nothing but praise for them. I asked some other workers standing nearby why this girl had so much love for the bosses. They laughed. 'Well, because she sleeps with the foremen,' one of them said. 'That's why she can get any job she wants. She just didn't feel like working today.'

"So you see," Sam continued, "under the hiring hall system, the worker does not have to sell himself. There is fairness and justice for all. A sense of dignity for the worker is always the most important gain in a struggle like this."

After I spoke to Sam, I drove north to Santa Maria. The strikers there had asked me to say a Mass for Cesar, who was still in the Salinas County jail. Over two hundred workers attended the service. When I told them what had happened to Ethel Kennedy at the Salinas jail, I could hear them gasp with horror and disgust. During the Mass, I emphasized the importance of Cesar's sacrifice in jail. I said that the growers in Santa Maria and Salinas would soon agree to negotiate with UFWOC. "But Cesar did not go to jail merely to get contracts and pay increases," I told them. "He wants to bring about changes in our society so that people will respect one another—so that men like Reagan and Agnew will find themselves out of office. If we stay united and dedicated to helping our brothers, then we can change this society. It will never be changed by money or by violence. It can only be changed for the better by nonviolent action and the spiritual power it generates.". . .

THE CHICANO MOVEMENT

A Basque priest, Father José Ellacuria, a Jesuit, accompanied me on a trip from Delano to Salinas. José, a slightly built man in his forties, had spent five weeks working in UFWOC's offices in Delano. He had familiarized himself with the workings of the union and the philosophy of Chavez. His plans were to develop some union leaders among Formosa's 34 million inhabitants. José had been in Taiwan for fourteen years.

As we drove through the long stretches of the San Joaquin Valley along Highway 99, we discussed the condition of the farm workers. José asked me about the federal subsidies given to the farmers. I explained that President Nixon had finally signed a bill into law limiting the amount of subsidies available to each farmer to $55,000. "The subsidies will eventually be eliminated," I added, "but there will still be many problems to tackle in the future.". . .

In Salinas, the sheriff would not permit us to visit Cesar. That evening, we joined Father Reynaldo Flores, a fellow Franciscan, and celebrated Mass in front of the jail. The workers had set up an altar on the back of a pickup, adorned with a cross, a painting of Our Lady of Guadalupe, and pictures of John and Robert Kennedy. They had been maintaining a continuous vigil since Cesar had been jailed. . . .

José and I stayed at a Franciscan retreat house at nearby San Juan Bautista that evening. Cesar and Helen had spent two weeks there in September, 1970, when Cesar was recovering from the effects of his second major fast. Since that time, the local growers had boycotted the retreat house and harassed the friars who reside there. But the fathers took everything in good spirits and looked forward to the time when they could again offer their hospitality to Cesar and his family.

On the following day, José and I paid a visit to an old friend, Ralph Guzman, a professor of Chicano studies at the University of California at Santa Cruz. The campus is nestled in the hills just above the blue Pacific Ocean. Ralph, dark complexioned, in his forties, and rather heavyset, with a round face and horn-rimmed glasses, greeted us enthusiastically and introduced us to his fellow instructors and to several Chicano students.

Ralph spoke enthusiastically of both the Chicano movement and Cesar's success with the farm workers. I asked him what the Chicanos in the cities thought of Cesar's movement.

"The militant Chicano leaders, like Denver's Corky Gonzales, have a great deal of respect for Cesar," Ralph said. "But very few Chicanos in the barrios are really acquainted with Cesar's ideas and techniques. For one thing, you must realize that life in the barrio street-corner society is violent. Things are very rough in the El Hoyo and Hazard districts of Los Angeles, for example. The people have to be tough to survive. The police, of course, are the most violent of all.

"So you see," Ralph continued, "if somebody starts theorizing about nonviolence, he just might be considered not very manly; *no muy macho*—in the language of the barrio.

"Who knows how successful Cesar could be, if he began to organize in the cities?" he added. "Things are so divided there, and there is so much rhetoric, so many shibboleths, yet very little organization. For years, many institutions have struggled for the minds of our people. The church, the Communist Party, the right wing, the government have all tried to influence our people. Maybe someone like Cesar could unite all the various segments of the Chicano community. One thing is certain—it would be one hell of a job."

Late that afternoon, I dropped José off at the University of San Francisco. He was to depart for Taiwan in two days. Luckily, I was able to contact Fred Ross, who now resides in San Francisco. Fred and his wife, Frances, live in a modest home in the hills above the Mission district. One can see the entire panorama of the city from their bay window.

AN INSIDER REFLECTS

Ross is a tall and lean man who looks younger than his years. The veteran organizer [from the Community Service

Organization (CSO)] leaves his hilltop home occasionally to aid Cesar during tough organizing campaigns. I had seen him many times during my stay in Delano and recently in Salinas. At present, he is working on a book dealing with his experiences as an organizer.

Fred concurred with me that the Salinas strike was probably the most successful field workers' strike in the history of U.S. agriculture. I asked him what direction he thought Cesar's movement would take.

"Organizing farm workers has been a very unpredictable situation," Fred stated. "The Delano strike began two or three years ahead of schedule. The Salinas strike was completely unplanned. The growers really set us up for that one."

Fred felt that Cesar's real task was to educate and politicize the farm workers. Many of them need citizenship, so that their voting power can have an effect on local and national politics.

"Many people regard you as the mastermind behind the whole movement, Fred," I said. Before I had finished the sentence, Ross answered with a firm "No, that's not true."

"Cesar received a few ideas and concepts from [Saul] Alinsky [founder of CSO] and me," he said. "But he developed his own philosophy and his organizing style. You know how well it has worked."

I asked about the difference between the styles of Alinsky and Chavez. "I think that the major difference is that Cesar has always been committed to the poor and always will be committed to the poor," he answered, in a serious tone. "Alinsky is now concentrating on the middle class. Besides that, Saul's technique as an organizer is to work with existing organizations in a community. Cesar's method has been to organize one person at a time. He has literally built his movement up from the foundations. He has worked like a bricklayer, carefully setting each brick in place."

"But what about the future of the movement?" I asked. "Many people say it will just become like any other union, that it will lose its family spirit and idealism."

"I don't agree with that point of view," Ross rejoined. "Cesar has injected his philosophy of mutual support and cooperation into his whole organization. From the very beginning, Cesar has educated the farm workers as to the significance of cooperatives and credit unions. He has made the farm workers aware of other groups and their problems, too."

I agreed with Fred that Cesar had placed the service-center aspects of his movement on an equal plane with his organizing drives. I recalled entire weeks during the winter months when Cesar had pondered ways to help the needy and even the nonfarm workers in the valley. He had already begun a special experimental school for children of farm workers, called the *Huelga* school. He had discussed plans to expand medical services through the farm workers' clinic. He had purchased a former TB sanatorium near Tehachapi and named it La Paz. La Paz is now UFWOC's cultural and nonviolent-training center. He had spoken to me enthusiastically about purchasing land for the Agbayani Village and about many other cooperative ventures for the poor of the valley.

Fred paused for a moment, as I prepared to leave. Then he smiled and said, "I used to tell Cesar to get his mind off Forty Acres and all those projects. But he insisted on developing his cooperative schemes, even if it meant diminishing his organizing efforts."

In my car, I turned on the radio. The news was typical—the latest gruesome details of the Tate-La Bianca murder trial and the My Lai massacre [in Vietnam.] As the newscaster began to relate [California] Governor Ronald Reagan's most recent ravings about the high cost, of welfare and medical care for the aged, I switched off the radio. My mind was elsewhere. I was thinking of Cesar, who was still in jail . . . and of dreams that were slowly coming true for thousands of farm workers.

Architect of a Movement

Cletus E. Daniel

In 1966 the AFL-CIO officially chartered the United
Farm Workers Organizing Committee; the successes
wrought by the fledgling union empowered a generation of migrant laborers. The struggle to achieve
their heightened status included the defeat of California Proposition 22, which would have all but banned
union organizing. In the workers' quest for improved
working conditions, Cesar Chavez was a galvanizing
force who served as a focal point of the movement.
He lived the doctrines of voluntary poverty and charity that he professed, and this won the respect of his
constituency. Cletus E. Daniel, professor of Industrial
and Labor Relations at Cornell University, attributes
Chavez's profound dedication to purpose as the key
reason for the union's successes.

The United Farm Workers Organizing Committee (UFWOC)
was formally chartered by the AFL-CIO in August 1966.

The public backing the farmworkers attracted, including
that of Senator Robert F. Kennedy, who became an outspo-
ken supporter of the union when the Senate Subcommittee
on Migratory Labor held its highly publicized hearings in
Delano during the spring of 1966, indicated that large segments of the American people believed that grape strikers
occupied the moral "high ground" in their dispute with farm
employers. To an important degree, however, public support
for the farmworkers' cause also reflected a willingness
among many Americans to believe and trust in Cesar Chavez
personally; to see in the style and content of his public "persona" those qualities of integrity, selflessness, and moral
rectitude that made his cause theirs whether or not they
truly understood it. And if Chavez was more embarrassed

than flattered by such adoration, he was also enough of an opportunist to see that when liberals from New York to Hollywood made him the human repository of their own unrequited idealism or proclaimed his sainthood, it benefited farmworkers.

"Alone, the farm workers have no economic power," Chavez once observed, "but with the help of the public they can develop the economic power to counter that of the growers." The truth of that maxim was first revealed in April 1966, when a national boycott campaign against its product line of wines and spirits caused Schenley Industries, which had 5,000 acres of vineyards in the San Joaquin valley, to recognize the farmworkers' union and enter into contract negotiations. For Chavez, who received the news as he and a small band of union loyalists were nearing the end of an arduous, but exceedingly well-publicized, 300-mile march from Delano to Sacramento, Schenley's capitulation was "the first major proof of the power of the boycott."

Chavez's tactical genius, and the power of a national (and later international) boycott apparatus that transformed an otherwise local dispute into a topic of keen interest and passionate debate in communities across the country, prompted one winery after another to choose accommodation over further conflict. For two of the biggest wine grape growers, however, the prospect of acquiescing to UFWOC's brand of militant unionism was so loathsome that they resolved to court a more palatable alternative: the giant International Brotherhood of Teamsters. And although they had no apparent support among farmworkers in the region, the Teamsters, under the cynical and opportunistic leadership of William Grami, organizing director of the union's western conference, eagerly sought to prove that theirs was indeed the type of "businesslike" labor organization which anti-union farm employers could tolerate. Yet as good as the idea first seemed to the DiGiorgio Fruit Corporation and then to Perelli-Minetti Vineyards, consummating such a mischievous liaison with the Teamsters proved impossible. In the end, neither the companies nor the Teamsters had the will to persist in the face of intensified UFWOC boycotts, angry condemnations by the labor movement, and a rising tide of public disapproval. The controversy was finally resolved through secret ballot elections, which resulted in expressions of overwhelming support for Chavez and UFWOC.

GRUELING VICTORIES

The victories won during the first two years of the Delano struggle, while they propelled the cause of farmworker organization far beyond the boundaries of any previous advance, left Chavez and his followers still needing to overcome table grape growers in the San Joaquin and Coachella valleys before the union could claim real institutional durability. The state's table grape industry, comprised for the most part of family farms whose hardworking owners typically viewed unionism as an assault on their personal independence as well as a threat to their prerogatives as employers, remained unalterably opposed to UFWOC's demands long after California's largest wineries had acceded to them. Thus when Chavez made them the main targets of the union's campaign toward the end of 1967, table grape growers fought back with a ferocity and tactical ingenuity that announced their determination to resist unionism at whatever cost.

While the boycott continued to serve as the union's most effective weapon, especially after employers persuaded compliant local judges to issue injunctions severely restricting picketing and other direct action in the strike region, the slowness with which it operated to prod recalcitrant growers toward the bargaining table produced in farmworkers and volunteers alike an impatience that reduced both morale and discipline. It also undermined La Causa's [the cause's] commitment to nonviolence. "There came a point in 1968," Chavez recalled, "when we were in danger of losing. . . . Because of a sudden increase in violence against us, and an apparent lack of progress after more than two years of striking, there were those who felt that the time had come to overcome violence by violence. . . . There was demoralization in the ranks, people becoming desperate, more and more talk about violence. People meant it, even when they talked to me. They would say, 'Hey, we've got to burn these sons of bitches down. We've got to kill a few of them.'"

In responding to the crisis, Chavez chose a method of restoring discipline and morale that was as risky and unusual as it was revealing of the singular character of his leadership. He decided to fast. The fast, which continued for twenty-five painful days before it was finally broken at a moving outdoor mass in Delano that included Robert Kennedy among its celebrants, was more than an act of personal penance. "I thought I had to bring the Movement to a halt." Chavez explained, "do something that would force them and me to deal with the whole question of violence and ourselves. We had to stop long enough to take account of what we were doing." Although the fast's religious over-tones offended the secular sensibilities of many of his fol-lowers, it was more a political than a devotional act; an in-trepid and dramatic, if manipulative, device by which Chavez established a compelling standard of personal sacri-fice against which his supporters might measure their own commitment and dedication to La Causa, and thus their al-legiance to its leader. The power of guilt as a disciplinary tool was something Chavez well understood from his study of life and philosophy of Gandhi, and he was never reluctant to use it himself. "One of his little techniques," Fred Ross said of Chavez's style of leadership, "has always been to shame people into doing something by letting them know how hard he and others were working, and how it was go-ing to hurt other people if they didn't help too."

Those in the union who were closest to Chavez, whatever their initial reservations, found the fast's effect undeniably therapeutic. Jerry Cohen, the union's able young attorney, while convinced that it had been "a fantastic gamble," was deeply impressed by "what a great organizing tool the fast was." "Before the fast," Cohen noted, "there were nine ranch committees [the rough equivalent of locals within the UFW's structure], one for each winery. The fast, for the first time, made a union out of those ranch committees. . . . Everybody worked together." Dolores Huerta also recognized the cura-tive power of Chavez's ordeal. "Prior to that fast," she in-sisted, "there had been a lot of bickering and backbiting and fighting and little attempts at violence. But Cesar brought everybody together and really established himself as a leader of the farm workers."

While a chronic back ailment, apparently exacerbated by his fast and a schedule that often required him to work twenty hours a day, slowed Chavez's pace during much of 1968 and 1969, the steadily more punishing economic effects of the grape boycott finally began to erode the confidence and weaken the resistance of growers. With the assistance of a committee of strongly pro-union Catholic bishops who had volunteered to mediate the conflict, negotiations between the union and the first defectors from the growers' ranks finally began in the spring of 1970. And by the end of July, when the most obdurate growers in the Delano area collapsed under the combined weight of a continuing boycott and their own mounting weariness, Chavez and his tenacious followers had finally accomplished what five years before seemed impossible to all but the most sanguine forecasters.

The union's victory, which extended to eighty-five percent of the state's table grape industry, resulted in contracts that provided for substantial wage increases and employer contributions to UFWOC's health and welfare and economic development funds. Even more important, however, were the noneconomic provisions: union-run hiring halls that gave UFWOC control over the distribution of available work; grievance machinery that rescued the individual farmworker from the arbitrary authority of the boss; restrictions on the use of pesticides that endangered the health of workers; in short, provisions for the emancipation of workers from the century-old dictatorship of California agribusiness. . . .

LEGISLATIVE SUCCESSES

Chavez demonstrated during the course of several legislative battles in 1971 and 1972 that his talents as a political organizer and tactician were exceptional. When the Oregon legislature passed an anti-union bill sponsored by the American Farm Bureau Federation, Chavez and his followers, in only a week's time, persuaded the governor to veto it. Shortly thereafter, Chavez initiated a far more ambitious campaign to recall the governor of Arizona for signing a similar grower-backed bill into law. And while the recall drive ultimately bogged down in a tangle of legal disputes, Chavez's success in registering nearly one hundred thousand mostly poor, mostly Chicano voters fostered fundamental changes in the political balance of power in Arizona.

It was in California, however, that the UFW afforded its opponents the most impressive demonstration of La Causa's political sophistication and clout, and Chavez revealed to friends and foes alike that his ability to influence public debate extended well beyond the normal boundaries of trade union leadership. With the backing of the state's agribusiness establishment, the California Farm Bureau launched during 1972 a well-financed initiative drive—popularly known as Proposition 22—designed to eliminate the threat of unionism by banning nearly every effective weapon available to the UFW, including the boycott. Having failed the year before to win legislative approval for an equally tough anti-union measure, farm employers were confident that they could persuade the citizens of California, as they had so often before, that protecting the state's highly profitable agricultural industry was in the public interest. Aware that the UFW could not survive under the restrictive conditions that Proposition 22 contemplated, but without the financial resources needed to counter the growers' expensive media campaign, Chavez and his aides masterfully deployed what they did have: an aroused and resourceful membership. In the end, the growers' financial power proved to be no match for the UFW's people power. In defeating Proposition 22 by a decisive margin—58 percent to 42 percent—the UFW not only eliminated the immediate threat facing the union, but also announced to growers in terms too emphatic to ignore that the time was past when farm employers could rely upon their political power to keep farmworkers in their place. . . .

In 1974 the union relentlessly lobbied the [California] state assembly to win passage of a farm labor bill providing for secret-ballot union-representation elections. Although it later died in the agribusiness-dominated senate, Chavez still demonstrated that the UFW had lost none of its political prowess. The union also brought considerable pressures to bear on Democratic gubernatorial nominee Jerry Brown to win a promise that, if elected, he would make the passage of an acceptable farm labor bill one of his top legislative priorities. The UFW had no real hope of achieving its legislative aim as long as the anti-union administration of Governor Ronald Reagan dominated the state government, but in the youthful Brown, who had actively supported the UFW's grape boycotts while he was a seminary student, Chavez recognized a potential ally.

Because they could not have the kind of explicitly anti-union law they had promoted through their unavailing campaign in support of Proposition 22, the state's farm employers, in a significant reversal of their longstanding position, sought to undermine the UFW by joining with both the Teamsters and AFL-CIO in support of federal legislation extending the National Labor Relations Act (NLRA) to include farmworkers. Chavez, who had years before supported such an extension, strongly opposed NLRA coverage for farmworkers both because of its diminished effectiveness in guaranteeing workers' rights and because it banned the secondary boycotts upon which the UFW had become so dependent.

With Brown's election in November 1974, a legislative solution to the conflict that had convulsed the state's agricultural labor relations for nearly a decade appeared to be at hand. But given the mutual rancor and distrust that existed between farm employers and Teamsters on the one hand and Chavez and his followers on the other, drafting legislation compelling enough in its composition to induce compromises required both unfailing patience and an uncommon talent for legerdemain. Brown, however, was persuaded that a combination of good will and resolve could produce such a "vehicle for compromise." The new governor recognized that almost ten years of constant hostilities had not only rendered the combatants less intransigent, but had also created public enthusiasm for legislation that might restore labor peace to California's fields and vineyards.

BIRTH OF THE ALRA

Though none of the parties affected by Brown's compromise bill was fully satisfied in the end, each found reasons to support it. For the Teamsters' union, whose reputation as labor's pariah was reinforced by its anti-UFW machinations, supporting the Agricultural Labor Relations bill was a belated act of image polishing. For the state's agribusinessmen, who were finally discovering that preemptive arrangements with the Teamsters would not protect them from the UFW's seemingly inexhaustible boycott organizers, accepting Brown's proposal promised to restore order to their long unsettled industry. For the UFW, whose leaders were hopeful that legislation might do for La Causa what it had earlier done for the civil rights movement, going along with the governor's bill was a calculated risk that had to be taken.

The Agricultural Labor Relations Act (ALRA), which went into effect during the fall harvest season of 1975, established a five-member Agricultural Labor Relations Board (ALRB) to implement the law, the most important provisions of which guaranteed the right of farmworkers to organize and bargain collectively through representatives chosen by secret-ballot elections. The ALRB, which faced problems not unlike those confronted by the National Labor Relations Board forty years earlier, was forced to operate under exceedingly difficult circumstances, particularly after disgruntled growers provoked a bitter year-long political confrontation with the UFW by blocking the special appropriations the agency needed to support its heavier than expected workload. Yet despite attacks from all sides, an inexperienced staff, and the administrative miscarriages that inevitably attended the discharging of so controversial and exceptional a mandate, the ALRB doggedly pursued the law's essential intention of ensuring that farmworkers were free to decide questions of union affiliation without undue interference.

Whereas Chavez was often frustrated by the ALRB's plodding pace and periodic bungling, and at times criticized its operation in language as caustic and intemperate as that used by the most aggrieved farm employer, he considered the law a "godsend . . . without question the best law for workers—any workers—in the entire country.". . .

But for the tenacious idealism and organizational virtuosity of Cesar Chavez, there is no reason to believe that the circumstances which fostered the ALRA's enactment would have arisen. Before he arrived on the scene, agribusinessmen in California were as secure in their power and authority as any employers in the country. Yet only ten years after Chavez and his followers first challenged their supremacy, farm employers were acquiescing to a law that augured the demolition of their one-hundred-year-old dominion over labor. . . .

THE QUEST FOR "RADICAL CHANGE"

As from the beginning, the UFW's future as an organization is inextricably linked to Cesar Chavez's success as a leader. And since 1975 the union's record testifies to a mixed performance on Chavez's part. After reaching a membership of approximately fifty thousand by the late 1970s, the union has slowly dwindled in size, comprising roughly forty thousand members by the early 1980s, nearly all of whom, except for isolated outposts in Florida, Arizona, and a couple of other states, are confined to California. The union's continuing failure to make greater headway among the 200,000 farmworkers who are potential members in California alone is attributable, in part, to the growing sophistication of employers in countering the UFW's appeal to workers through voluntary improvements in wages and conditions; to the entry into the farm labor force of workers without strong emotional ties to or knowledge of the heroic struggles of the past; and to the inability of an increasingly politicized ALRB to enforce the letter and the spirit of its mandate in a timely fashion, especially following the election in 1984 of a governor allied with the union's fiercest opponents.

It is also the case, however, that the UFW's drift from vitality toward apparent stagnation is partially rooted in a web of complex factors related to the sometimes contradictory leadership of Cesar Chavez: a sincere devotion to democratic unionism that is undermined by a tendency to regard all internal dissidents as traitors at best and anti-union conspirators at worst; a professed desire to make the UFW a rank-and-file union governed from the bottom up that is contradicted by a strong inclination to concentrate authority in his own hands and those of close family members; a commitment to professionalize the administration of the UFW that is impeded by a reliance on volunteerism so unyielding as to have caused many of the union's most loyal and efficient staff members to quit.

In fairness, however, Chavez's performance must be assessed on a basis that encompasses far more than the normal categories of trade union leadership. For unlike most American labor leaders, who had stood apart from the traditions of their European counterparts by insisting that unionism is an end in itself, Chavez has, in his own somewhat idiosyncratic way, remained determined to use the UFW and the heightened political consciousness of his Chicano loyalists as a means for promoting changes more fundamental than those attainable through collective bargaining and other conventional avenues of trade union activism. In defining the UFW's singular mission, Chavez once declared: "As a continuation of our struggle, I think that we can develop economic power and put it in the hands of the people so they can have more control of their own lives, and then begin to change the system. We want radical change. Nothing short of radical change is going to have any impact on our lives or our problems. We want sufficient power to control our own destinies. This is our struggle. It's a lifetime job. The work for social change and against social injustice is never ended."

When measured against the magnitude of his proposed enterprise, and against his extraordinary achievements on behalf of workers who were among the most powerless and degraded in America prior to his emergence, Chavez's real and alleged deficiencies in guiding the UFW across the hostile terrain of California's industrialized agriculture in no way detract from his standing as the most accomplished and far-sighted labor leader of his generation. Whether or not he has it in him to be more than a labor leader, to turn the UFW into an instrument of changes still more profound and far-reaching than it has already brought about, remains to be proven.

The history of American labor is littered with the wreckage of workers' organizations—the Knights of Labor and the Industrial Workers of the World among them—that tried and failed to combine the immediate purposes of trade unionism with an ultimate ambition to alter the fundamental structure of American society. Indeed, in an era when many labor leaders are preoccupied with nothing so much as the survival of their organizations, Chavez's pledge before the UFW's 1983 convention to lead the union in new and even bolder assaults against the economic and political status quo seems distinctly unrealistic. Unrealistic, that is, until one recalls the implausibility of what he has already accomplished.

The Violent Resistance to Change

Jacques E. Levy

Because Chavez's goals for the union were broader
in scope than traditional industrial unions, United
Farm Workers supporters often referred to their
struggles as *La Causa* or "The Cause." Biographer
Jacques E. Levy traveled with Chavez in the early
1970s and kept a reporter's notebook on events as
they happened. In these excerpts, Levy recalls the violent grower and anti-unionist reactions to Chavez
and his efforts. These passages also record the hundreds of arrests of striking workers and others sympathetic to *La Causa.* Levy is author of the seminal
work *Cesar Chavez: Autobiography of La Causa.*

On July 10, 1973, the nation's largest winery, Gallo Brothers,
which has had a contract with UFW for six years, signs a
four-year Teamster contract.

After signing, the company announces that its workers
voted 150 to 1 for the Teamsters, but at the time, all but 27 of
its regular workers are on strike.

Earlier, Gallo refused to hold elections, despite UFW re-
quests.

Gallo then tries to evict from its labor camps some sev-
enty families who have been with the company up to fourteen years. The families, with four hundred children, are
striking UFW members.

Franzia winery also refuses to renegotiate its UFW contract. So does White River Farms, formerly owned by Schenley. There, after the workers strike, the company has no
workers in the field for nine days. But 288 arrests and imported strikebreakers help break the strike. . . .

July 21, 1973—*Los Angeles Times* news item: The Kern
County Sheriff's Department sought to relieve the jail crush

Jacques E. Levy, *Cesar Chavez: Autobiography of La Causa,* New York: W.W. Norton,
1975. Copyright © 1975 by Jacques E Levy. Reproduced by permission.

two days ago by releasing about 120 pickets who had been arrested for the first time. But in a show of solidarity, the first arrestees refused to sign citations and leave the jail unless all their companions went with them.

Similar tactics were used by UFW members in Fresno County, where deputies arrested 885 persons at Five Points, Parlier, and Reedley.

Sheriff Melvin Willmirth reported that the pickets refused to accept citations, as 452 arrested the day before had done. He said yesterday's arrestees were demanding to be jailed....

The same week ... Kern County deputies charge the picket line one morning on Edison Drive by the Giumarra ranch. They use their billy clubs and mace.

Seventeen-year-old Marta Rodriguez, a small, slender girl, has her arms pinned and twisted behind her and is dragged by deputies across the street into an orchard. Terrified by the brutality all around her, she screams in terror.

Frank Valenzuela, former mayor of Hollister and now an organizer with the American Federation of State, County and Municipal Employees, goes to her aid. He offers to take the hysterical girl to a police car to calm her, but officers converge on him, strike him in the legs, spray mace in his eyes, then hit him in the stomach. They pin his arms behind him, shove his face into the ground, and arrest him.

Five-foot-tall Harriett Teller, twenty-three, who is on the scene as a legal aide to the union, is pushed with a police club and maced as she tries to take pictures.

Tomas Barrios of Coachella, a picket captain, is jumped on by Teamsters and police rush in. Four deputies grab him, one with a strangle hold, and he is choked until he passes out. Then he is arrested, and the Teamsters are let go.

Other pickets have their hands handcuffed behind them and are beaten. The police helicopter swoops low to scatter the pickets by spraying dirt clods in their midst. In all, 230 pickets are arrested, including three Jesuits.

WORKERS VOTE TO STRIKE

On July 21, some two thousand union supporters and farm workers march through Delano and hold a rally in the park to impress on Delano growers the strength of the union. Their contracts expire Monday, July 29.

The following week, about two thousand farm workers gather at Forty Acres [union hall] and vote to strike if the Delano growers don't sign a new contract by midnight Sunday.

Bill Kircher promises them support. "I'm here to tell you the same thing I told you in 1965—that the working people of the AFL-CIO are with you, and we'll stay with you. This is Delano. This is the heart of the union, the core of the farm workers movement, and there isn't a power on earth that can destroy it."

July 29, 1973—At the Ramada Inn in Bakersfield, the negotiations between UFW and the Delano growers recess at 3:30 A.M. Eight hours later, the two dozen farm workers return to the conference room and wait for the growers to appear. Unless the impasse is broken in the next few hours, they face another painful strike. They sit silent, serious, and tense.

Suddenly Cesar leaps up on the negotiating table, facing the growers' empty chairs. He arches his left arm upward while stretching out his right—thrust, parry, thrust. In the best swashbuckling style of Errol Flynn, he shadow fences his enemy.

"This is Zorro," he jokes as he goes through his pantomime. The farm workers smile and relax, their tensions eased.

But when Giumarra and the others file in, the talks go nowhere. John Giumarra, Sr., complains of a headache. He didn't sleep an hour, he says, his eyes half-shut. He can't take aspirin. He has an ulcer. "You need guts of steel, and that's not good enough. You need stainless steel," he comments.

They get down to business, but fifteen minutes later the talks collapse. "If you change your position you can call us," says the growers' attorney.

"You have our phone," Cesar counters.

"Huelga!" [strike] shout the workers as they file out. . . .

July 30, 1973—The Delano table-grape pickers leave the vineyards and set up their picket line. After three peaceful years, the long strike for their own union is resumed.

August 1, 1973—More than forty priests and nuns from throughout the U.S. are among three hundred pickets arrested in southeast Fresno County. The number of pickets in the three San Joaquin counties is estimated by deputies at some three thousand.

In Delano, UFW picket Joe Moncon, eighteen, is shot in the right shoulder while getting into a car near the Tudor ranch vineyards. The shotgun blast is fired from a truck passing the picket line. There are no arrests following the shooting. . . .

ARRESTS AND THREATS

August 2, 1973—Several hundred farm workers are in the city park in Parlier when Cesar arrives at dawn. He tells them of the plans to continue mass arrests, to fill the jails in defiance of the injunctions.

In the background is [social activist] Dorothy Day, looking frail but determined, her militancy undiminished after seventy-six years. Yesterday she was on the picket lines at the Giumarra ranch in the Arvin-Lamont area hoping to be among those arrested. But there were no arrests. So this morning she has traveled one hundred miles north to Fresno County where the mass arrests are continuing.

When Cesar is through talking, she walks up to him, holding her cane whose handle opens into a seat.

"Say a prayer that this time they'll take me," she asks Cesar.

"I will," Cesar answers.

He, too, decides to be arrested, but first he must call a number of people in the union to alert them. By the time he completes his calls and reaches the picket line, it is gone. All have been arrested. He searches out another line, but again arrives too late. His attempt fails.

Dorothy Day, however, is jailed. . . .

The union sends its doctors and nurses to give the prisoners health checks. They find three workers whose TB [tuberculosis] check is positive, but Fresno County officials refuse to do anything about it. Two others have high blood pressure and one a bad heart, but the county refuses to release them without bail.

The jailers prohibit the nuns, Jesuits, and other religious representatives from holding daily mass on the grounds they might get drunk on the wine. They also refuse to let the nuns have mosquito repellent on the grounds they might sniff it and get high.

When Cesar visits the county industrial camp, one moving scene follows another. Each time he enters a men's barrack, the imprisoned workers crowd around him, embrace him, and cheer. But the most moving scene is in the women's barracks where Dorothy Day is housed.

"Don't waste your time in jail!" he tells the women, whose spirit seems even more militant than the men's. "You should have classes twice a day."

Addressing Dorothy Day he says, "Tell them the story of

the labor movement," and turning to the nuns he says, "Tell them about the life of a nun."

In a lighter vein he comments, "The sisters' network is really humming these days! I'd hate to be a judge!" When the laughter dies down, he says, "You should pray for Judge Pettit. You're in heaven compared to him."

"What's happening here is no different than what happened in Selma" [referring to the bus boycott organized by civil rights leader Martin Luther King Jr.] he says. "It's truly a blot on the conscience of America."

Juanita Escarano, a Sanger farm worker, is one of several who express their feeling about being in jail. She steps up on a wooden table that has become a makeshift platform. "It's very evident we're very happy to be here because this is the best way to win the struggle," she tells her fellow prisoners and Cesar. "This kind of spirit can't be jailed."

August 4, 1973—In Tulare County, the sheriff's tac squad tries to incite Juan Cervantes, a nineteen-year-old picket captain, into a fight, but the youth keeps his cool. Back at the Forty Acres he describes to Cesar what happened at the Dispoto ranch.

As he yelled "Huelga!" at the scabs, a deputy snarled, "If you don't keep your mouth shut, we'll take care of you, you four-eyed monkey."

Another officer threatened, "Don't worry. We've got your license plate. We'll kill you."

"Are you threatening me?" Cervantes asked.

"You can call it what you want," the cop answered. And the racial insults and threats continued.

August 7, 1973—About 250 pickets are massed on the north side of the huge Giumarra vineyards in Lamont. Several dash into the vineyards to talk to the strikebreakers who are deep in the vineyard.

Kern County deputies spot them and rush in, but instead of arresting them, they beat them with their clubs.

Anger spreads through the picket line, and the picket captains, to cool things off, call off the pickets and move them to neutral ground on the railroad tracks.

Giumarra's security guards and the deputies soon have them flanked on the north, east, and west. When an officer orders them to leave the track area, a picket captain tells him they have a right to be on the private property unless requested to leave by the railroad.

Again police order them to move, but the pickets instead kneel down to pray. Then the police charge, their clubs flailing, their mace canisters spraying.

As the workers panic and flee toward their cars, they find that police have them surrounded. They must charge through the police lines to escape, ducking both the clubs and the mace.

Among those badly injured is forty-three-year-old Ernestina Ramon who is struck across the eye by a club, and AFL-CIO organizer Joe Lopez from New York.

A number of pickets prevented from getting to their cars by police are forced to walk miles back to union headquarters.

[Social radical] Jerry Cohen recalls: The vast majority of the arrest cases were dismissed. Most of them were for violating an injunction or for unlawful assembly. There were a few assorted charges—like people would throw dirt clods, several threw rocks, and there were some in for assorted scuffles.

But when you think that 3,589 people were arrested, I think well over 3,400 of those were clear First Amendment issues and had nothing to do with even alleged disturbing the peace or stuff like that. So it was an amazing performance by the farm workers. They really kept their cool when they were attacked.

And that shows, in the words of that justice in the Massachusetts Supreme Court, how the courts have been acting as a cavalry in the employers' army by issuing those injunctions. Because what happens is the arrests effectively inhibit strike activities.

CHAPTER 3

STRATEGIES AND TACTICS OF AN ORGANIZER

PEOPLE
WHO MADE
HISTORY

CESAR CHAVEZ

Plain Speaking and "House Meetings"

Fred Ross

Social activist Fred Ross played a pivotal role in
Cesar Chavez's apprenticeship as a labor leader, and
continued to work with Chavez for many years.
From Ross, Chavez learned valuable organizational
strategies, such as taking his message directly to the
workers he hoped to help in the form of "house
meetings." These gatherings would take place at the
homes of the workers instead of the larger organizing halls traditionally used by industrial unions. In
this excerpt from his memoirs, Ross recalls his initial meeting with a skeptical Chavez and their first
collective efforts.

In the late spring of 1952, I had come to San Jose to build a
chapter of the Community Service Organization. The C.S.O.,
as we called it, was a civil rights-civic action movement
among the Chicanos with, at that time, the reputation of being the most militant and effective organization of its kind in
the United States. I had just completed the organization of
the mother-chapter in East L.A., and was bringing word of
its wonders to the East Side of San Jose and to the home, that
night, of a young man named Cesar Chavez.

But I was about the last guy Cesar Chavez wanted to meet
in the tough eastside San Jose barrio they nicknamed "Sal Si
Puedes" (which translates "get out if you can"). It was where
Cesar and his family often called home since they began life
as migrant farm workers in the late 1930's. Cesar was ten
when the bank foreclosed on the small family farm his
grandfather had homesteaded during the late 1880's in the
Gila River Valley outside Yuma, Arizona.

Many of the people who lived in Sal Si Puedes worked in
the orchards and vineyards which then flourished outside of

Fred Ross, *Conquering Goliath: Cesar Chavez at the Beginning,* Keene, CA: El Taller
Grafico Press, 1989. Copyright © 1989 by El Taller Grafico Press, United Farm Workers of America. Reproduced by permission.

town. It seemed that the only way young men left Sal Si Puedes was to go off to jail, the military or the cemetery. Cesar was then laboring in apricot orchards outside San Jose, where he had come to settle after getting out of the Navy at the end of the war. . . .

So then we started the housemeeting. I told Cesar and his buddies I had worked all over Southern California. And wherever I went the conditions among the Mexican Americans were as bad as in Sal Si Puedes. The same polluted creeks and horse pastures for kids to play in. The same kind of cops beating up young guys and "breaking and entering" without warrants. The same mean streets and walkways, and lack of street lights and traffic signals. The same poor drainage, overflowing cesspools, and amoebic dysentery.

Cesar was impressed. He realized I knew his problems as well as anyone. I didn't rabble-rouse; I just talked quietly about what I had done helping the people of Riverside and Redlands, in the Casa Blanca and El Modena barrios, do away with segregation in the schools and skating rinks and schoolbuses. And how, on the eastside of Los Angeles, the people built their own civic-action organization (the C.S.O.), which went to work on their problems as well as registering neighbors to vote and turning them out to the polls.

I told them about the C.S.O.'s response to "Bloody Christmas 1951," when seven young Chicanos were nearly beaten to death by drunken cops. And how never before, in the whole history of Los Angeles, had any cop ever gotten "canned" for beating up a Mexican American. If the people of Los Angeles could do it, I said, there was no reason why we couldn't do the same sort of thing in Sal Si Puedes, if we wanted to badly enough. . . .

The day after that meeting at his house, Cesar had come out to head up the first voter registration drive ever held in the barrio. Others fell by the wayside, but Cesar had ploughed right on through for forty consecutive nights, achieving a final total of over four thousand newly registered Chicano voters.

THE "HELSTEIN PLAN"

The following year, I convinced my boss, Saul Alinsky, head of the Chicago-based Industrial Areas Foundation (I.A.F.), to hire Cesar. For the next ten years, we worked together, organizing C.S.O. chapters in all of the major barrios in California. We led drives that registered over 500,000 Chicanos to vote, brought U.S. citizenship and old-age pensions to approximately 50,000 Mexican immigrants, fought for installation of paved streets, sidewalks, traffic signals, recreational facilities and clinics, and forced a drastic curb on police brutality and "urban removal" of Spanish-speaking residents from redevelopment projects in many of those same barrios.

Then, one day, the wire from Saul Alinsky came, calling Cesar and me to San Francisco to meet with him, Ralph Helstein, head of the United Packinghouse Workers of America (U.P.W.A.), and Tony Rios, national president of the C.S.O., to discuss the "Helstein Plan."

The Helstein Plan called for the U.P.W.A. to join forces with the C.S.O. in establishing a pilot project which, if successful, could set the groundwork for launching a national farm workers' movement. Oxnard was selected as the starting point because of its heavy Chicano farm worker population and because the union already had a base there in the fruit and vegetable sheds.

This joint union-C.S.O. organizing plan evolved at the height of the bracero farm labor program. The United States government had begun importing bracero farm workers from Mexico to work mostly in Southwest agriculture because of alleged labor shortages brought on by World War II. But growers liked the compliant and underpaid braceros so much that they managed to extend the program after the war ended, even though the labor shortage had passed. During the 1950's and early '60's, hundreds of thousands of foreign field laborers were imported to work on U.S. farms, including the citrus- and vegetable-growing region around Oxnard.

The pilot project was to be a sort of hybrid C.S.O. It would encompass the usual functions of an ordinary C.S.O. chapter, but its major concern would be with the farm workers through development of a Farm Worker Employment Committee, infinitely stronger and more effective than those in any of the other chapters.

At the "appropriate point" in its history (presumably when sufficient "union consciousness" had been developed among its members), this committee would sever its connection with its mother-C.S.O. and attach itself to a new "host," the union.

Of not inconsiderable importance to the C.S.O., which was then struggling to obtain financial self-sufficiency, was the promise that the United Packinghouse Workers would sweeten the pot to the tune of twenty thousand dollars, provided Cesar agreed to do the job.

"Jesus! Fred," Cesar exclaimed, "I didn't let on but I didn't know what in hell to say when they offered me that job. In one way, I was gung-ho to do it. But at the same time, there was this fear thing—like, maybe I'm asking for too much, and what if I fail—that kept creeping in. You know how it is. Over the years you hear those little things about how good you are. Of course, you don't believe them at first. But they sound good. So after a while you start believing them a little bit. Well, quite a bit, I guess.". . .

Cesar had finally taken the job. Then, at the insistence of the C.S.O. board, he and Helen and the seven kids had gone to Carpenteria State Beach ten miles north of Oxnard so he could get a little rest before beginning the work.

THE KEY TO ORGANIZATION

Cesar had tried to relax, but every time he started to let go, the thought of that twenty thousand dollars, along with the nebulous dimensions of the new job, had tightened him up again. He had always been paid, of course, while he was working with me and Alinsky. But there the salary, such as it was, had come from the rich. Now it would come directly from the workers. And that was different. . . .

"Gee, Fred!" he said, ". . . I keep wishing so hard that someone would come along and give me the 'Key' to this whole damned thing I'm saddled with. One of those great organizing plans: Roman Numeral I and then Capital A, that sort of thing. Something to tell me how I'm going to get to the farm workers, for one thing. But also to show me what this line is that I'm supposed to go up to, and then stop and turn the whole thing over to the union."

The more he had thought about it the more charged up he got, until finally, on the pretext of looking for a place to rent in Oxnard, he slammed out of there and went into the little town to see if, maybe, somehow, just being with the people would help him find the "Key."

The Colonia hadn't changed much since he was there as a migrant kid tying carrots with the family twenty years before. There was Juanita School, where the kids used to bug him every day for wearing the same old clothes—the only ones he had. The old shack was still there, where they had pitched the tent the day they first landed in town. It had been raining that night, he had recalled, and he and his brother, Richard, had reached out through a hole in the tent and caught the rain in their hands.

But some things had changed. On the western edge of the Colonia, blocking what had once been the main entrance and exit way, was a huge sugar factory. He had heard how they had tricked the Chicanos into voting for it by telling them an underpass would be put in as soon as they got the factory built. That had been five years ago, and still no underpass. Without it, a Colonia home could burn to the ground before the firetruck reached the scene from the firehouse across town. . . .

From there, Cesar had gone over to check the action at the United Packinghouse Workers Union. Their office was a storefront on the bottom floor of an old, two-story building. Upstairs was a chop suey joint and next door a drive-in they called the Blue Onion.

The office was in two parts. In the back was a small, partitioned-off space where a woman was typing and a man was working a mimeograph machine. The front was empty except for four or five rows of folding chairs.

"So I go in there, Fred," he said, "and stand by one of the chairs watching them. The woman looks up and keeps right on typing. Pretty quick the guy slows up the mimeo crank and turns to me: 'What can we do for you?' he wants to know.". . .

In the next few minutes, a small crowd gathered in the office and Cesar went into his pitch. It was the same old rap he had always used—the way C.S.O. had been able to help the Chicanos build power all over California. They could do the same thing in Oxnard, he told them, providing the people were willing to bear down and work with him. He said nothing about the union or the problems of the farm workers. Straight C.S.O. But when he finished, the workers were so impressed a number of them stepped forward, unsolicited, to help him get the organization rolling.

"What it is, Fred," he said "these people are some of the 'cream' more or less. They just naturally want to get together and fight for their rights. Until I got there with C.S.O., there was no place else to go but the union. Now, hearing about C.S.O. they can see it is the thing they had wanted all along.". . .

Next day, Cesar started the "housemeeting" organizing drive. The idea was simply to persuade one person at a time in the Colonia to invite a few friends, relatives, and neighbors to the house to meet with Cesar. This would give him a shot at convincing them, under the most favorable circumstances, to join C.S.O. It was also an ideal way of drawing people out, getting them to discuss things that were bothering them and, in the process, to sell themselves and each other on the value of the organization.

Most important of all was the "crunch." This came at the end of the housemeeting, and was the point at which Cesar had to convince the guests to invite people to their home to meet with him. By never failing to "crunch" people at succeeding housemeetings, Cesar was able to build a solid chain of small meetings, leading, at the end of four or five weeks, to a large, Colonia-wide organizing meeting. At that time, he would call together all of the people he had met at the housemeetings and form the Oxnard C.S.O.

Righteous Rhetoric

John C. Hammerback, Richard J. Jensen, and
Jose Angel Gutierrez

John C. Hammerback, chair of the California State
University, Hayward, Department of Mass Commu-
nications, and Richard J. Jensen are the coauthors of
several studies on the rhetorical strategies of Cesar
Chavez. Jose Angel Gutierrez is an associate professor of political science at the University of Texas at
Arlington. According to the authors, "Chavez relied
on public communication to change the established
order." The authors argue that while Chavez's
speeches attracted a broad audience, it was his clarity of speech and righteous rhetoric that persuaded
his audiences effectively. This selection is excerpted
from *A War of Words*, cowritten by John C. Hammerback, Richard J. Jensen, and Jose Angel Gutierrez.

In the early spring of 1962, thirty-five-year-old Cesar Chavez
moved from San Jose to Delano, California, to begin organizing farm laborers into an effective union, a task most labor leaders considered impossible. California farmworkers
typically had been illiterate, indigent, and migratory, and
growers had easily broken all farmworkers' unions since
1903. Further diminishing Chavez's chances of success, he
initially lacked co-workers, personal wealth, political power,
or formal education past the seventh grade. The son of migrants and a former crop-picker, he appeared to be no
match for the wealth and power of California agribusiness.

As most successful reformers in American history have
done, Chavez relied on his public communication to change
the established order. During his first eleven months in Delano the 5'7", 150-pound laborer worked in the fields all day
and then drove to farmworkers' camps and homes almost
nightly, attending "hundreds of house meetings" while canvassing for members in eighty-seven communities within

John C. Hammerback, Richard J. Jensen, and Jose Angel Gutierrez, *A War of Words*,
Westport, CT: Greenwood Press, 1985. Copyright © 1985 by Greenwood Publishing
Group, Inc. Reproduced by permission.

about a 100-mile radius. Luis Valdez, founder of El Teatro Campesino, remembered that Chavez entered Delano as neither the "traditional bombastic Mexican revolutionary; nor was he a *gavacho*, a gringo, a white social worker type," the two types who previously had tried and failed to organize the Mexican-Americans and Filipinos who comprised the majority of farm laborers in the area. "Here was Cesar," Valdez explained, "burning with a patient fire, poor like us, dark like us, talking quietly, moving people to talk about their problems, attacking the little problems first, and suggesting, always suggesting . . . solutions that seemed attainable. We didn't know it until we met him, but he was the leader we had been waiting for."

Chavez's talking led to tangible accomplishments. By 1965 he had established a union with more than 2,000 dues-paying families. His United Farm Workers (UFW) soon offered precedent-setting services ranging from a newspaper and credit union to health clinics and old-age benefits, and by 1972 UFW membership passed 30,000 and had affiliated with the powerful AFL-CIO. UFW victories included strict agreements regarding the growers' use of pesticides which endangered workers; contracts with "most major wineries, the lettuce-growing subsidiary of United Brands, and the citrus-growing subsidiary of Coca Cola" and the nation's first collective-bargaining legislation for farmworkers. Chavez's crusade, featuring strikes, marches, fasts, and speeches, established his reputation as a charismatic leader and won for the UFW statements of support ranging from the mayor and city council of San Francisco to the 1972 Democratic national platform. Although the UFW temporarily lost contracts when the powerful Teamsters Union challenged it in a bitter battle to represent farmworkers, a settlement with the Teamsters in 1977 established the UFW as the sole bargaining organization for crop-pickers in California.

ATTRACTING A BROAD AUDIENCE

As Chavez attracted national attention, he gained a reputation as "the most persuasive union leader to come along in a generation." Although he expanded his audience to the entire nation, he maintained the dogged persistence in speaking that had typified his earlier canvassing for farm laborers. Nearly exhausted during a speaking tour in 1965, he addressed a college audience from which he was pelted by eggs and tomatoes. The weary Chavez scarcely noticed the flying food and continued calmly presenting his case—and the audience applauded him for his apparent coolness. On a three-month tour in 1969 of some ninety cites in the United States and Canada, he reported that "everywhere I spoke I asked people to get hold of their Congressmen and make a complaint. And you know, it worked." In 1972 a co-worker complained that Chavez loved to organize workers, "but he can't do it because right now he has to go around speaking." Listeners to the slender but energetic Chavez, a man with "an Indian's bow nose and lank black hair, with sad eyes and an open smile," included congressional committees, college students, political gatherings, Christian organizations, viewers of the national news media, and even Pope Paul VI. Among those early moved by Chavez's persuasion was Dolores Huerta, who later became a leader in the UFW. After initially perceiving him as quiet and shy, she "heard him speak one time at a board meeting and . . . was really impressed."

Chavez served as a major Chicano leader as well as a union leader. From its beginnings the UFW was closely identified "with the civil rights movement and its techniques of aggressive nonviolence." Consisting mainly of Mexican-Americans, his farm labor movement played a major role in creating the Chicano protest. Although Chavez frequently emphasized union interests over ethnic issues, he became the most prominent, most revered, and only nationally recognized leader of Mexican-Americans. Chicano poet Octavio Romano V gave Chavez credit for teaching the lesson that "the Mexican-American must state his case before the entire nation and stir its conscience." The non-violent activist became a folk hero for many Americans of all colors and the "spiritual leader for Chicanos" during the turbulent 1960s. A wide variety of Americans shared the opinion of him expressed in *Look* magazine: "At a time when many American radicals are saying that nonviolence—as an instrument for social change—died with Martin Luther King, it is reassuring to meet a man of faith who preaches compassion rather than bloody confrontation, practices what he preaches, and gets results." On ABC television's "Good Night America," host Geraldo Rivera described Chavez as "one of those really rare people, who qualifies under the heading of legend in their own time." This legend grew from speeches like the one he delivered at the federal prison at McNeil Island, after which the president of the Chicano prisoners group exclaimed: "This man has brought us this dream. He has given us reason to say: 'I'm an American of Mexican descent, and I am proud of it.'" A perplexed Teamster president Jimmy Hoffa expressed a less flattering view of the idealistic Chavez: "Sure I like the guy. But he's some sort of religious fanatic in search of martyrdom. You can't run a union that way."

Chavez's reliance on discourse and his ability to appeal to a broad audience, to reach "the campesino and college student alike," characterized his rhetorical campaign. . . .

BACKING WORDS WITH BELIEFS

The roots of Chavez's view of public discourse have been in his perceptions of God and reform and in his experience as a labor organizer. A devout Roman Catholic, he described the worldwide ecumenical church as "one form of the Presence of God on Earth" and a "powerful moral and spiritual force" in the world. He has accepted orthodox Catholic positions; for example, the Church must care for the poor, and Christ's model of non-violence is admirable. . . .

As a union organizer, Chavez developed a millennial interpretation of contemporary history based on his beliefs in God, the injustice suffered by the poor, the need to organize workers, and the power of public address. As the 1960s ended, he declared: "People are not going to turn back now. The poor are on the march: black, brown, red, everyone, whites included. We are now in the midst of the biggest revolution this country has ever known." With the UFW consisting primarily of disadvantaged members of racial minorities, Chavez viewed union issues as civil rights issues which pitted the strong and rich against the poor and weak. Therefore the UFW, he instructed, was "not just another union," but a movement "to change the conditions of human life." To Chavez, then, the UFW was "a family bound together in a common struggle for justice." His convictions that "our cause is just, that history is a story of social revolution, and that the poor shall inherit the land," led him to announce with assurance: "We will win, we *are* winning, because ours is a revolution of mind and heart, not only of economics." Just as irreconcilable labor-management disputes can often be settled by an impartial third-party arbiter, he envisioned a human arbiter of his struggle for justice: public opinion. Convinced that "the love of justice in the hearts of other Americans is still our last and best hope," he confidently forecasted: "I contend that not only the American public but people in general throughout the world will respond to a cause that involves injustice.". . .

His Oral Delivery

Throughout Chavez's rhetorical career his oral delivery—his use of voice and body—reinforced his persona as a gentle advocate who emphasized content over personality. Biographers reported that his speeches were "soft, sweetened by a Spanish accent" and that "what is striking in his gentle voice is his lack of mannerisms." The London *Times* noted that he "overwhelmed the listener with his gentleness." Protestant Minister Winthrop Yinger, who heard Chavez speak "three or four dozen times" between 1965 and 1976, described his "conversational tone of delivery. He does not punctuate his ideas with shouts; indeed, he seldom raises his voice at all." Speaking slowly and deliberately, calmly and gently, Chavez appeared to trust the persuasive power of his arguments and explanations.

Chavez's non-verbal communication extended past his delivery. In a well-publicized protest march in 1966 from Delano to the state capitol in Sacramento, for example, farmworkers walked under the banner of the Virgin of Guadalupe as well as the flags of Mexico and of the farmworkers. In the view of [authors Matt] Meier and [Feliciano] Rivera, the symbolic appeal of the Virgin of Guadalupe attracted Mexican-Americans to Chavez's organization. Chavez himself understood the appeal of the symbol. He explained that the basilica of the Virgin of Guadalupe was the major shrine in Mexico for pilgrims, many of whom walked on their knees during the final mile or two. "Made with sacrifice and hardship as an expression of penance and of commitment," this trip often included a request to the patron for benefits "of body or soul." Thus, the Mexicans' religious pilgrimage paralleled that of protesting farmworkers who also offered their suffering and commitment to a moral cause in which they expected success.

Righteous Rhetoric

Chavez's discourse . . . contained distinctive features. He employed lucid explanations and arguments, illustrated with plentiful facts, simple anecdotes, and concrete examples. He added clarity to his case through abundant transitions and a simple style. Elevating his message and himself above purely practical, pragmatic, or selfish interests, he stressed moral issues and treated opponents generously. His case for supporting his union fit into his broader argument that racial minorities, in particular Mexican-Americans, were being swept ineluctably by Providence toward the economic, social, and political justice they deserved. His calm delivery further focused attention on his message rather than on himself. Not neglecting rhetorical concerns, he adapted his topics to immediate audiences and pressing issues. These same characteristics emerged in numerous other speeches and formed his rhetorical profile.

Chavez's discourse persuaded Anglos as well as Mexican-Americans. For Chicanos, he employed conventionally powerful patterns, forms, and appeals: folksaying and *dichos* or maxims; anecdotes and stories or *cuentos*; Spanish formality, graciousness, and respect, as illustrated by his warm and respectful acknowledgments in introductions; and familial and religious themes and images, which surfaced in his references to God and his examples of and quotes about Mexican, Mexican-American, and southwestern families. On occasion his allegiance with the Virgin of Guadalupe further linked his cause and calls to action with the religion and culture of Mexican-Americans. To Anglo idealists in the idealistic 1960s, moreover, he was also an ideal spokesman—one with a case built on abundant facts and high moral principles. That case, because it was presented so calmly and clearly, appeared to trust the good judgment of right-minded listeners regardless of color.

Chavez's rhetorical posture as a calm teacher of truth may be unusual for an ethnic activist or militant labor organizer, but it is not surprising in light of his conception of rhetorical discourse. Influenced by his experiences as a labor organizer and by his views of religion and reform, he saw himself as playing a crucial role in God's plan to right injustices suffered by the poor. The temporal means to these divine ends was the American public which, when well informed, would effectuate appropriate reforms. His job was not primarily to inspire militant action on a particular issue but to educate audiences about farmworkers' moral struggles and tactics. Hence, he relied on facts and clarity, focusing on the power of his ideas rather than on his personal accomplishments, and he avoided vilifying opponents or haranguing audiences, preferring to let his explanations and arguments speak for themselves. Influencing the quantity as well as the quality of his public address, his faith in the ultimate success of his morally right rhetoric motivated him to present his case persistently despite awesome obstacles to success. In the end, Chavez's victories may have justified his faith in righteous rhetoric.

Emphasizing Morality and Nonviolence

Matt S. Meier and Feliciano Rivera

Cesar Chavez continued his fight for basic worker necessities (such as death benefits for those who could not afford to bury their loved ones) in the 1960s, a time when civil rights issues were center stage in American politics. Chavez's philosophy of nonviolence resonated with civil rights activists across the country, and political leaders seized the opportunity to ally themselves with the moral issues of justice and equality espoused by union leadership. Matt S. Meier and Feliciano Rivera have written on the Chicano movement and its key participants. In the following piece from 1972, they argue that Chavez, through his efforts, augmented the social and economic viability of California's agricultural workers. Meier is professor emeritus of history at Santa Clara University.

[Chavez's] organization, today known as the United Farm Workers' Committee (UFWOC), is more nearly a coöperative than a union and incorporates earlier ideas of nineteenth-century Mexican mutualist organizations. Within its structure, it has developed for its members a death benefit plan; a coöperative grocery, drug store, and gas station; a credit union; a medical clinic; a social protest theatre group, the Teatro Campesino; and a newspaper, *El Malcriado*. Furthermore, the UFWOC has extended its efforts beyond helping farm laborers and concerns itself with problems affecting the broader Chicano community, providing a unifying force in the struggle for Chicano civil rights.

Chávez patiently established locals in the southern San Joaquin Valley, and in two years the National Farm Workers Association (NFWA) had 1,000 members. . . . César Chávez and the NFWA completely molded and dominated the [1965] Delano grape strike. Chávez felt that the strike had possibilities of success because of the termination of Public Law 78 and the bracero program in 1964, plus the relatively large core of active union members living in the Delano area. He viewed wages and collective bargaining as only part of the strike's objective, which, in a broad fashion, was intended to restore human dignity to farm workers. Skillfully using America's response to the civil-rights movement of the 1950s and early 1960s, he dramatized the farm worker's plight by presenting the grape strike as a broad movement for social justice.

APPEALING TO THE AMERICAN CONSCIENCE

Chávez carefully developed the strike movement on two basic principles, nonviolence and the use of outside help. Realizing that outsiders were more able and ready to stand up against pressures than local people, he made full use of a wide range of civil-rights and religious groups. In September 1965, he visited Stanford University and the University of California at Berkeley and invited both individuals and organizations (such as the Congress of Racial Equality and the Student Nonviolent Coördinating Committee) to take part in the struggle. As a result of these visits, a steady stream of students, ministers, nuns, priests, and civil-rights workers came to Delano; many went back to spread the Delano story on the campuses and in the cities.

Religion played and continues to play an important role in Chávez' struggle. The symbolic invocation of the Virgin of Guadalupe attracted Mexican Americans to the NFWA and also had the effect, when coupled with the prestige of the California bishops of the Catholic Church, of making the usual accusations of Communism seem ridiculous. In March 1966, Bishop Hugh Donohoe of Stockton, testifying before the Senate Subcommittee on Migratory Labor in Delano, read a position paper signed by all seven California bishops. This statement upheld the farm workers' right to organize and strike and called for legislation to bring farm labor under the National Labor Relations Act as a first step in settling farm labor conflicts.

State and national political leaders, notably Governor Edmund G. "Pat" Brown and Robert Kennedy, played an important part in the strike movement from its inception. Support also came from various labor leaders, union organizations, and prominent Americans like Mrs. Martin Luther King, Jr. Most important, however, was Chávez' strategy of always viewing and presenting the strike as a moral issue, thereby appealing to the American conscience. . . .

CHAVEZ THE TACTICIAN

The strike received wide support from various labor organizations and other groups. The San Francisco Labor Council began sending monthly motorcades of food and clothing to Delano; and in December, after an appearance and talk in Delano, labor leader Walter Reuther began sending $5,000 a month to support the strike. . . .

However, many difficulties arose in carrying out the strike. Picketing thirty-five ranches in an area of 400 square miles presented an organizational problem of staggering proportions; another immense problem was that, throughout the strike, local officials were clearly on the side of the growers. Violence developed—mostly, but not entirely, on the growers' side. Chávez' insistence on nonviolence kept the strike remarkably free from serious outbreaks. However, strikers often found their tires deflated; and trucks, dusting machines, tractors, and spray equipment became weapons in the growers' fight against the NFWA. Local police feigned difficulty in discerning grower violence but moved quickly to arrest strikers for being "ready to violate the law," as Kern County Sheriff Roy Galyen testified before the Senate Subcommittee on Migrant Labor. Futhermore, when arrested, union pickets found their bail high, while growers usually were released on their own recognizance.

By the end of 1965, the three-month-old strike had had little result, and Chávez decided on the strategy of pitting Schenley Industries' national interests against its Kern County interests by organizing a nationwide boycott of Schenley. With this . . . strategy helping to focus national attention on the strike, sixteen NFWA organizers were sent to principal cities throughout the United States to set up boycott programs. From the standpoint of publicity, the most successful of these was in Boston, where a Boston Grape Party was staged, complete with lugs of grapes being dumped into Boston harbor.

Early in 1966, Chávez decided to march on the state capital at Sacramento, a move planned to involve state politicians in the Schenley boycott and to dramatize the grape

THE DECISION TO FAST

In February 1968 Cesar Chavez embarked on what would turn out to be a twenty-five-day fast. Author Winthrop Yinger regards the fast as both an act of moral protest and an attempt to organize workers.

> Nonviolence exacts a very high price from one who practices it. But once you are able to meet that demand then you can do most things, provided you have the time. Gandhi showed how a whole nation could be liberated without an army. This is the first time in the history of the world when a huge nation, occupied for over a century, achieved independence by nonviolence. It was a long struggle and it takes time.
>
> —CESAR CHAVEZ

This speech delivered at the conclusion of the twenty-five-day fast of Cesar Chavez was an affirming speech. It was not so much a speech to convince as it was one to reaffirm fundamental Union goals. It was a speech calling farm workers to a unity of direction and to purposeful action. Its positive appeal is for a life style that is nonviolent, the underlying premise being that violence is weak and immoral and will shatter a cause or movement. . . .

The occasion for the speech was a critical time in the Union's history. In his Good Friday Letter Chavez alluded to this fact.

> Knowing of Gandhi's admonition that fasting is the last resort in place of the sword, during a most critical time in our movement last February, 1968, I undertook a 25-day fast.

strike. With about sixty NFWA members and supporters, on March 17 he began the 300-mile, 25-day walk which brought them to Sacramento on Easter Sunday. As they neared the capital, news reached the marchers that Schenley had agreed to accept the NFWA as the bargaining agent for its 450 vineyard workers, to use the NFWA instead of labor contractors, and to pay $1.75 per hour. Following this success, Christian Brothers, which earlier had suggested to other growers that collective bargaining had arrived in the vineyards, also signed an agreement with the NFWA. . . .

CHAVEZ DECIDES TO FAST

In August, 1967, Giumarra Vineyards, Inc., one of California's largest table-grape growers, became the new target of UFWOC. Giumarra insisted that its workers were happy

The Union cause was grinding away so slowly that the spirit of the movement was being charged with tension and frustration. The possibility of violent eruption was very high. That being true, the occasion for this speech was also a time of personal crisis for Cesar Chavez, for his life is inexorably wedded to the farm worker movement.

One critical question remains unanswered: Was the fast a pure moral act or an internal organizational device? It is clear that the fast was undertaken at a time when the internal dissension problems were critical and the general morale of the Union was extremely low (due largely to the draining effects of the boycott efforts, threats and acts of violence, and because there had not been a decisive victory for a relatively long period of time). It is also clear that Chavez is a sincerely religious man and fasting is no stranger to him. Furthermore, Chavez's two chief nonviolent mentors, Gandhi and Martin Luther King, also practiced fasting. The question of motive, however, still remains.

The surface evidence supports an inclusive response to the question; that is, the fast was *both* a personal, moral act and a human model in organization commitment. Part of the purpose of the fast was to bring together divergent, frustrated commitments in UFWOC's membership. The Union also needed a persuasive, catalytic example of sacrifice for the cause, as well as a symbolic victory. Chavez's fast apparently gave the farm workers both.

Winthrop Yinger, *Cesar Chavez: The Rhetoric of Nonviolence,* 1975.

without a union; however, it increased its use of greencarders [imported Mexican labor] to work in the fields. As the Delano grape strike continued, with Giumarra as its principal focus, Chávez became concerned about a loss of spirit and a rising mood of violence among his followers. In February 1968, Chávez began to fast as a symbolic act of rededication to the principles of nonviolence. After twenty-five days his fast ended, but the struggle with Giumarra continued. The union now charged that scab greencarders formed a large percentage of Giumarra's work force and that the company habitually shipped grapes under other growers' labels. Giumarra's subsequent admission of using both greencarders and labels other than its own led to a table-grape boycott which spread all across the country and even abroad. . . .

On July 29, 1970, the five-year struggle came to an "end"

when Giumarra and twenty-five other Delano grape growers, producing about 50 percent of California table grapes, signed a three-year contract with UFWOC. This agreement, again mediated by the Bishops' Committee on Farm Labor Disputes, was hailed by both sides as the beginning of a new era in labor relations in California agriculture. During the ensuing victory celebration, Chávez announced that UFWOC's next target would be the Salinas Valley lettuce growers.

Whatever the outcome in the Salinas Valley, Chávez' efforts brought to an end the growers' assumptions that agricultural workers are a happy, contented lot who do not want the benefits of union organization. Furthermore, farm labor organization has changed the social and economic structure of California agriculture, and it can never return to its old patterns.

The Role of Rituals

J. Craig Jenkins

The challenges faced by Cesar Chavez demanded
sacrifice on his part and solidarity on the part of the
workers he hoped to represent. His deft integration
of religious practices, such as fasting and Easter
peregrinations (or pilgrimages) expertly dramatized
his struggles as issues of social justice. Ohio State
University sociology professor J. Craig Jenkins argues the invocation of traditional Mexican and
Catholic rituals unified field workers and framed
their struggle as issues of morality.

The strategy for mobilizing the Farm Workers Association
drew on the two organizing traditions in which Chavez had
been schooled: the multi-issue community organizing
model developed by Saul Alinsky and Fred Ross, who had
founded the Community Service Organization (CSO); and
the mutual benefit associations of the Catholic Church, most
directly represented by the Spanish Mission Band's Agricultural Workers Association. Chavez drew selectively on both,
borrowing organizing tactics from the former and programs
from the latter. Of these, Ross was the most important influence. Although trained by Alinsky, Ross had developed a
slightly different organizing approach. Alinksy had organized the Back of the Yards Movement in settled working
class neighborhoods surrounding the old stockyards in
Chicago on the assumption that the neighborhoods had sufficient resources and indigenous organization to support a
challenge. The key problem was creating an awareness that
the neighborhoods were excluded from city politics and that
urban elites were exploiting their exclusion. Organizing was
primarily a question of building formal associations, typically by forming alliances among existing groups, and using
confrontation tactics to reveal elite exploitativeness. The organizer was purely a catalyst, initiating the challenge and

J. Craig Jenkins, *The Politics of Insurgency*, New York: Columbia University Press,
1985. Copyright © 1985 by Columbia University Press. Reproduced by permission.

then withdrawing to allow the community to direct its own fate. In contrast, Ross contended that the Mexican immigrants were sufficiently disorganized and without leaders that an open challenge would immediately collapse. First, they had to develop solidarity ties, indigenous leaders, and a tradition of pooling resources. Organizing was a question of developing solidarity, training indigenous leaders, and creating new organizations. The organizer had to make a long-term commitment, investing years and perhaps a decade before open challenges would be possible.

SOLIDARITY AND SACRIFICE

The organizing tactics that flowed from this approach proved extremely effective. Because solidarity was so central, Chavez held house meetings at which supporters invited friends and neighbors to their homes to discuss solutions to local problems. Organizing automatically zeroed in on the more settled, cohesive farm workers and made use of bloc recruitment. Chavez also tried to be a friend to all the workers, Association members or not, taking personal interest in their lives and any problems they brought to his attention. . . . Friendship was a selective solidarity incentive that helped create networks of solidarity and, at least until the Association became too large, strong ties to Chavez himself. The Association also held festivals and parades on religious and civic holidays and used Catholic and Mexican symbols to stir the workers. If anything could generate instant solidarity among the Mexican immigrants, it was the Virgin de Guadalupe at the head of a procession or a festival on Cinco de Mayo, the anniversary of Mexican independence. Chavez also insisted that the workers had to be willing to sacrifice for the collectivity, and he deliberately set Association dues high, at $3.50 a month, with little tolerance for late dues. . . . The point was to instill a morale of sacrifice and commitment to la causa. Throughout the initial organizing, there was no talk of a union or strikes. Not only might this intimidate the workers, but it would alert the growers and prompt the attention of local police and courts. The strategy was to prepare a basis for a union, not organize a union outright. Chavez also followed Ross' advice on staff. Professional organizers had to make a long-term commitment, and since the aim was to create indigenous leadership, volunteer organizers would come only from the farm workers. He also borrowed the Catholic vow of voluntary poverty, requiring professional staff to accept a subsistence salary of housing and food plus $5 per week for personal spending. Commitment was total, often requiring 80–100 hours' work a week and, as the organization grew, communal living arrangements.

Chavez also drew on the mutual benefit associations of the Catholic Church. The basic notion here was solving immediate life problems and generating a sense of community. By providing selective incentives like low cost credit, health services, and cooperative buying and collective incentives through festivals and celebrations, the Association solved the farm workers' most immediate problems and created a sense of solidarity. Once immediate problems had been addressed and a base of solidarity created, the farm workers would be prepared to deal with larger problems. . . .

IMMEDIATE CONCERNS

Chavez spent the winter and summer of 1962 making contacts throughout the Valley under the pretext of conducting a social survey of the colonias. By leaving postcards to be filled out on which the workers could express their desires, Chavez identified potential supporters and learned more about the workers' immediate concerns. He later followed up these leads with house meetings at which he revealed the plans for a benefit association. Soon he had a long list of small-scale projects that could address immediate concerns. If a family member died, few of the workers had sufficient savings for a funeral. The Association would offer a funeral benefit fund. Most had trouble getting by during the winter and could not secure credit at the local banks to buy cars or houses. The Association would organize a credit union. Because the workers had to drive long distances to work, keeping a car in repair was a major expense. The Association would organize a gasoline co-op and buy tires and supplies cooperatively. Many workers were trying to obtain citizenship and clearance for a relative to move to the United States or to collect welfare payments. The Association would provide immigration counseling, set up citizenship classes, and intervene with welfare agencies.

By September 1962, the FWA had a membership of 300 families and several thousand contacts. Chavez decided to call a founding convention in Fresno for September 30. Around 250 supporters showed up, ratifying the proposal to create the Farm Workers Association and Richard Chavez's Aztec black eagle flag as the Association symbol. Benefits were initially limited to a burial insurance plan and a credit union, with plans for a gasoline co-op, counseling services, and eventually a health care center. Over the next two years, Chavez patiently kept organizing, living off donations by members, his brother's support, and a small salary. By 1964 the Association had over 1,000 members and a well-established credit union administered by Helen Chavez with $25,000 in assets. Yet the Association was still an extremely limited operation, with only Chavez as full-time professional staff and fewer than a dozen volunteer organizers. . . .

Although Chavez had vowed to stay out of direct challenges to growers, he soon led the Association into several skirmishes. By the spring of 1965, the Association had over 1,500 families and had several small successes to its credit, having doubled the registration of Mexican-American voters and initiated complaints against a racist teacher and several growers for payroll abuses. In early April, several Association members who worked in the Mt. Arbor rose nursery near McFarland got embroiled in a pay dispute with the manager. . . .

In early May several crews of Filipino grape harvesters organized by the four Agricultural Workers Organizing Committee (AWOC) Filipino organizers—Larry Itliong, Philip Vera Cruz, Andy Imutan, and Ben Gines—struck in the Coachella grape harvest, demanding the bracero minimum of $1.40. . . .

AN INDEPENDENCE DAY VOTE

The Association confronted a dilemma. If it joined the strike, it risked three years of preparatory organizational work. On the other hand, if it ignored the strike, it violated its commitment to the farm workers. At first Chavez temporized, running stories in the Association paper *El Malcriado* ("the bad boy") urging members to respect the AWOC picket lines. But the Mexican strikebreakers continued to walk across the lines. When FWA members began to join the parade, Chavez called on Itliong to discuss possible cooperation, and after considerable staff debate, Chavez announced a meeting to discuss joining the strike.

On Thursday evening, September 16, 1965, Mexican Independence Day, an enthusiastic crowd of over 1,200 overflowed the parish hall of Our Lady of Guadalupe Church. While Chavez was still skeptical about the strike, the crowd was enthusiastic, and the staff and student radicals supporting the strike carried the day. They decorated the walls with posters of Emiliano Zapata, the Mexican revolutionary hero, and Jack London's definition of a strikebreaker as "a two-legged animal with a corkscrew soul, a water-logged brain and combination backbone made of jelly and glue." A huge huelga ("strike") banner graced the rostrum with the Association's black eagle in the center. Speaker after speaker roused the crowd, reminding them of their Mexican revolutionary heritage. "Viva la Huelga! Viva la Causa! Viva Cesar Chavez!" came the reply. When Chavez finally asked for a strike vote, the hall broke out in a unanimous "Huelga! Huelga! Huelga!" The FWA would join the AWOC.

Chavez asked the members to wait until the following Monday, the 20th, so that the Association could contact the growers, organize picket teams, and finalize their alliance with the AWOC. Reflecting the new aspirations, the Association also adopted a new name: the National Farm Workers Association (NFWA). . . .

The major problem was the workers' poverty. Many sympathized with the strike but felt they could not afford to pass up the harvest wages. The NFWA had only a few hundred dollars in the treasury and could not pay strike relief. The Association called on members to donate food and housing, but they could not handle the entire load. Over 2,000 individuals, workers and their families, passed through the Delano headquarters during the first week. Soon the pickets began asking new supporters to simply move on to jobs outside the strike zone. The AWOC paid strike relief and the Filipinos gave solid support, but they were only a third of the normal workforce.

Then Chavez had a stroke of genius. The growers had secured a court injunction restricting picket teams to five at each ranch gate and bans on any disturbance of the peace. The sheriff had told his deputies that any mention of "huelga" or use of loudspeakers constituted a disturbance. Chavez decided to turn adversity to an advantage, using the restrictions on their freedom of speech to appeal for outside support and renew sagging strike morale. David Havens volunteered to test the injunction by reading Jack London's famous definition of a strikebreaker for the enjoyment of the sheriff's deputies. The deputies immediately arrested Havens, providing the strikers with a protest issue. . . .

THE EASTER MARCH

The picket teams were beginning to grumble, and as the last truckloads of grapes were hauled off, they had no more fields to picket. To give them something to do, Chavez ordered two workers and a student volunteer to trail a shipment of Schenley grapes to the Oakland docks in hopes of keeping it from being loaded. . . . To everyone's amazement, the pickets persuaded the longshoremen at the dock to refuse to handle the hot cargo. Schenley Corporation immediately demanded an injunction, but before the labor arbitrators could make a decision, the ship had to depart. Over 1,000 ten-ton cases of grapes sat rotting on the Oakland wharves. . . .

In no time, the boycott had caught hold.

Dateline: Los Angeles. Sympathetic students leaflet liquor stores and clear the shelves.

Dateline: San Francisco. Retail Clerks and Teamsters demand that management pull Schenley off the shelves.

Dateline: New York. Government workers, 5,000 strong, pledge to boycott Schenley liquor. Union leaders picket Schenley headquarters.

Dateline: Boston. Civil rights militants hold a Boston Grape Party to spread the boycott.

Dateline: Oklahoma City. Local priests picket liquor stores, demanding Schenley be removed.

The boycotters also organized actions against the table grapes. Student volunteers followed shipments of "scab" grapes leaving the strike area for distant markets. Sympathetic railwaymen recorded the destinations of cars, giving the pickets an opportunity to catch up with the shipments. In the neighboring Roseville switching yard, the NFWA pickets surrounded a carload of grapes, and sympathetic railwaymen sidetracked the shipment for several days while it rotted under the broiling sun. . . .

Still the challenge did not have teeth. Morale was low, and although the boycott was still on, there were no signs of a breakthrough. With no crop activity, there was not even anything to picket. Someone suggested a mass march across the country to imitate the 1963 March on Washington. Scaling the suggestion down to size, Chavez suggested an Easter perigrinacion, a Catholic procession of Lenten penitence.

The march was to begin in Delano, with the destination Sacramento on Easter morning. . . .

The march created an opportunity to renew contacts and assure supporters that it was only a question of time before la huelga would come to their area too. As the procession neared each town, runners were sent ahead to prepare for a festival. When the marchers entered towns, they were met by a local delegation who furnished food and housing for the night. Each night a rally was held for the workers, and each morning the march began with a Mass. Bill Kircher of the AFL-CIO was impressed:

> The march was an organizing tool. New. Radical. Different. A crew of our people walking along the highway carrying the banner of Our Lady, calling meetings at night which attracted farm workers out of the fields and towns, opening with "De Colores" [a song used by the lay Catholic Cursillo movement that spoke of the colors of spring in the fields], maybe a prayer. The whole thing had a strong cultural, religious thing, yet it was organizing people.

The 300-mile march gave sympathizers a rallying point. Priests, Protestant clergy, students, and radical unionists flocked to the closing days. As the procession advanced on Sacramento, it swelled from seventy-five *originales* to over 5,000. . . .

On Easter morning the ragtag marchers triumphantly moved on the state capitol in Sacramento. At the head of the swelling column was a Mexican worker, his sombrero bent against the sun, brandishing a velvet and silk tapestry depicting Our Lady of Guadalupe, the patron saint of Mexico. Behind him marched over 5,000 workers, students, unionists, priests, and ministers. Some bore scarlet and white banners, their black thunderbird emblems snapping in the dusty breeze. Others waved signs: "JUSTICE FOR FARM WORKERS! GRAPES OF WRATH 1936–1966! VIVA LA HUELGA!"

Centralized Management

Susan Ferriss and Ricardo Sandoval

Several prominent defections from the union in the 1980s led to speculation that trouble was brewing within union leadership. Although many who left the union were hesitant to criticize Chavez in public, the perception that Chavez was a stubborn taskmaster fueled debate on the necessity of a strong centralized union without local representation. When the media entered the fray, the union found it difficult to face the ever-present new political challenges amidst the internal turbulence. Susan Ferriss and Ricardo Sandoval discuss the union's decline in the following article.

Cox Newspapers correspondent Susan Ferriss is both a journalist and documentary filmmaker. Ricardo Sandoval writes for the *San Jose Mercury News.*

At the beginning of 1980, after nearly two decades of nonstop organizing, Cesar Chavez's drive to change farmworkers' lives had yielded an embarrassment of riches. With the hard-won victories in the lettuce fields of the Salinas and Imperial Valleys, membership in the UFW, according to a union count, surpassed a hundred thousand. The unionized *lechugeros* in California were probably paid at the highest rate of any American field laborers. With the new contracts and the increases in piece-rate pay, the fastest workers could earn up to twenty dollars an hour at the peak of the lettuce harvest, rivaling wages in nonfarm manufacturing. Moreover, the contracts included benefits and vacation packages previously unheard of for farm laborers. For the workers themselves, other crucial benefits of union membership were starting to materialize as well. The medical plan, built up by funds from growers who had signed the new contracts, was reaching more and more workers.

Farmworker elections sponsored by the American Labor Relations Board (ALRB) were also becoming regular events, despite seemingly never-ending battles with growers in Sacramento and in state courts. On forty-six ranches in California, most of them stretching across the coastal vegetable empire near Salinas, farmworkers voted to join the union. . .

As growers were regrouping, the union's accomplishments made it tempting to move on to new challenges. Rumors even sprang up that Cesar was considering stepping down as UFW president. But these stories were quickly explained by [union spokesman] Chris Hartmire. "We've been working more on a management team concept to share the leadership, to take more of the responsibility," Hartmire told a reporter in 1982. Underneath Hartmire's public position, however, was an intensifying debate that for several years had centered on questions about the future of the union: Was it to be a social movement led by Chavez? Or was Cesar just the chief executive of a traditional labor union? The answers were almost as varied as the number of people working at La Paz.

A STUBBORN TASKMASTER

Some former union members say Chavez liked delegating authority and routinely created opportunities for inexperienced staff members who showed promise. He was especially patient with young staff members who came from farmworker families. Marc Grossman remembers that Cesar would sometimes bark out an order, but then back off to see how the task was carried out: It was his way of keeping an eye out for future union leaders. Others remember Cesar could also be a stubborn taskmaster, and there were few events that took place at La Paz or within the union without Chavez's direct oversight. He was tirelessly engaged. Al Rojas recalls that he'd fire off directives about almost every aspect of union business, sometimes in a curt manner that would unsettle people who didn't know him. In one instance Cesar personally "handled" one staff member's excessive phone use by climbing over a desk to pull out the phone cord; another time he ordered Rojas to take back a union credit card and a car from a young lawyer who had racked up huge business and travel expenses, and not to accept an explanation.

During this period, Cesar touched off a brushfire by selecting inexperienced staff members for the union's first training class for labor-contract negotiators, funded by the AFL-CIO and taught by Fred Ross. "There were some who thought we should go out and get college-educated kids and get them into this program, but Cesar also wanted to give a chance to young [farmworker] staffers, who'd had fewer opportunities in life. He wanted to test them and see if they'd respond," Grossman remembers, adding that Miguel Contreras, who in the 1990s became the first Latino to head the powerful Los Angeles County Federation of Labor, was in the first graduating class of that training program. Though Chavez wanted the union to mature, he also wanted the union's future leaders to come from the same stock as its original farmworker members.

At times, Chavez's personality puzzled his coworkers: his strong desire to delegate was at war with an equally strong need to retain control. Unlike most trade unions, the UFW did not have local branches, or units, which would hold elections of union representatives. This disappointed UFW members who equated autonomy with union democracy. Rather than a simple rejection of autonomy, however, Chavez's position reflected a goal he had written into the union's first constitution twenty years earlier: The UFW would be a strong centralized union with no locals. In writing that first constitution, Cesar reasoned that a migrant workforce made local branches impractical, while a central union with many far-flung district offices would allow farmworkers on the migrant trail to vote, get help, or file grievances wherever their field work might take them. . . .

IRRECONCILABLE DIFFERENCES

As spontaneous as this struggle over union control seemed, it was really nothing new. As far back as the Delano grapestrike days, resistance to a strong central leadership was evident. Doug Adair remembers that in the 1960s, the freethinking staff of *El Malcriado* created a list with their own names and gave each other demerits when someone would preface an order with "Cesar says . . ." When the union was young and individual roles were still evolving, those differences appeared harmless, even mildly amusing. But as the union matured, divisions over leadership, as well as goals, grew deeper and threatened the stability of the movement.

Adair traces some of the problems to the fame that enveloped Cesar after his initial fast in 1968. Before the fast Chavez "was our leader, but he was our brother. . . . But after the fast he had a role to play on the national stage. After 1968 it was very difficult, certainly for me, to disagree with him, because he had this tremendous moral stature and authority. And you couldn't go in and tell him anymore, 'Cesar, you're full of shit. That's a terrible idea.' . . . In a sense, [his fame] separated him from the other brothers and sisters. It put him on a pedestal . . . and according to him it was not of his choosing. It made it harder for him to really listen, which is what he was best at. And there was no other organizer in the union who was as good an organizer as Cesar. He was the best. He was tops.". . .

The tumult was underscored by the departures in 1981 of Marshall Ganz and Jessica Govea, both highly regarded organizers who disagreed with Chavez on the direction of the union; Ganz, in particular, felt the UFW was not doing enough to support the union's grassroots field organizing. UFW attorney Jerry Cohen also left in 1981, on good terms with Chavez but unhappy with the controversy, which, he felt, was hobbling the union. Growing personal and philosophical differences also ended the longtime friendship between Chavez and Gilbert Padilla, who felt that he had to leave once the union leadership considered him "not a team player." The departures hurt and angered Chavez. *La causa* was all-important to Cesar; he admitted that he had given up his private life for the UFW. Although it was not expressed publicly, former union aides said that, to a degree, Chavez expected others to do the same. "There is no life apart from the union," Chavez once told a reporter. "It is totally fulfilling."

Most of the people who left the union talked respectfully afterward about Cesar and muted their criticism of the UFW in public. But privately, some gave vent to their dismay, charging that the union had become disorganized, with conflicting orders and shifting strategies. Former union supporters complained about an inconsistent stream of orders from La Paz—a centralized management that, they said, stifled local organizing. . . .

MEDIA ENTERS THE FRAY

As the Union's turnover and internal dissension undermined its ability to organize the growing farmworker population, critics seized on the UFW troubles. In 1979, Chavez had qui-

etly endured a critical article in the *New York Times* portray-
ing him as an autocrat who had fallen from grace. The re-
porting that followed was often characterized by glaring errors as well as its reliance on innuendo and anonymous
sources. In 1984 the *Village Voice* ran a series on Chavez, who
was described as a tyrant with a "mirthless grin." The story
described a litany of internal battles and portrayed union
leadership as a virtual cult borrowing from Synanon and wor-
shiping Cesar. But the worst media attacks came from NBC
News in 1979 and a column by muckraker Jack Anderson in
1980 that echoed the network's story. "It saddens me to have
to report," Anderson wrote, "that the United Farm Workers
(UFW) union, which lifted so many stoop laborers out of pe-
onage and degradation, has become a violence-prone, tyran-
nical empire under the ironfisted rule of Cesar Chavez. . . ."

The article levied a series of charges against Cesar, and
quoted former union members, including Tony Orendain,
who claimed the UFW had strayed from its original mission.
The column further charged that Cesar and his closest followers were raising large sums of money with the help of
celebrities like Joan Baez, but not using it to help farmworkers and organizers. Moreover, Anderson wrote, Chavez had
stood by as an "investigative reporter" was "badly beaten" at
a union meeting in Arizona.

The allegations outraged Cesar, and he turned to famed
San Francisco lawyer Melvin Belli for advice. Within a
month, Belli had sent a letter to each of the newspapers that
had published Anderson's column, refuting the major allegations. Reexamining the genesis of his report, Anderson
found that his researchers had gotten their facts seriously
wrong. Anderson sent another reporter to La Paz for a meeting with Cesar, and in a stunning mea culpa, wrote:
"Flanked by three lawyers dressed in three-piece suits, a
fuming Chavez sat in the hot California sun tearing clumps
of grass from the ground as he spoke. He was angry. . . . But
he was also persuasive."

The reporter and victim of the alleged assault, a friend of
rival farm-labor organizers, told investigators from the
union and Belli's office that he had not been beaten, and that
Cesar probably never knew that he was in the audience. A
priest, whom Anderson had credited with rescuing the reporter, also refuted the story. The union also showed Anderson's researchers stacks of financial documents that tracked

more than a decade of fund-raising and revealed that the money had been used as strike benefits and seed money for organizing efforts not only in California, but in Arizona and Texas as well. . . .

PUBLIC ACRIMONY

Public exoneration wasn't enough, however, to keep the UFW's internal rift from widening, and it came to a head at the union's 1981 convention in Fresno. Salinas field representatives claimed that Chavez was avoiding their pleas for help in setting up a local credit union and for adequate support staff to handle the long new union rosters and a flood of claims for medical benefits. They also complained that the UFW board had too many college-educated members, who were unfamiliar with the difficulties of farmwork. In an attempt to have their own voice on the union's board of directors, the Salinas representatives nominated three candidates to run against officers who had been put on the ballot by the union's leadership. It was an unprecedented and miscalculated challenge: There was clearly not enough support for the Salinas candidates. When word started passing among delegates of an attempted coup d'état by the Salinas faction, Chavez responded by blaming the attempted rebellion on "external forces." (Rumors circulated on the convention floor that the dissidents had been put up to this test by Ganz—part of his plan to carve out a breakaway union based in Salinas. A saddened Ganz denied he had tried to usurp power.) The Salinas faction walked out of the convention, and its leaders were subsequently fired.

Chavez's retaliation only worsened the problem. The seven field representatives, elected by their peers from Salinas-area farms, filed a lawsuit against the union for wrongful termination. In his defense, Cesar insisted that the representatives had actually been appointed by the union's leadership, and that the workers' vote was not the final word. In 1982, a judge sided with the Salinas contingent, saying the UFW had violated labor rules by firing the elected representatives, awarding them back pay and jobs at unionized farms. One of the fired representatives, Sabino Lopez, says he is not sure to this day why he was fired and refuses to discuss the incident, except to say that it was the darkest time of his life.

The public acrimony left the union vulnerable. Labor analysts began to suggest the union had abandoned its field-organizing efforts, and that by losing veteran leaders like Padilla, Ganz, and Govea, critical outreach work was being left to younger staff members with little experience. Sensing problems within the union, growers became even more recalcitrant. Many farmers skirted the union by hiring fewer laborers directly, instead turning to the network of unscrupulous labor contractors who filled fields with undocumented Mexican immigrants. The growers' legal strategy was increasingly successful, and they filed challenge after challenge against successful ranch-organizing drives and union elections. In 1982 the number of new elections at ranches fell to twenty-one, including several union-decertification attempts. . . .

NEW POLITICAL CHALLENGES

After the overtly pro-grower George Deukmejian was inaugurated [as governor] in 1982, he appointed David Stirling as ALRB general counsel. Stirling, an unsuccessful candidate for state attorney general, was on a mission to tilt the law away from what he saw as a "pro-union bias," and by 1983, the union started seeing a lot of its painstaking organizing work go to waste.

"There's no question that the standard we are applying to cases is much more stringent," said Stirling, shortly after taking office. "In the past, it is my belief that complaints would go forward that were simply not justified and should have been settled or not gone at all."

Union complaints that growers interfered with elections, fired pro-UFW workers, and refused to bargain for new contracts after elections went largely unheeded by the ALRB in 1983. Chavez complained bitterly that the labor board was preventing the union from gaining new members because of delays in investigations and certifications. Early into Deukmejian's first term as governor, the agency nearly imploded. While Chavez's organizers were trying to coalesce workers into voting blocs, ALRB lawyers and field representatives were quitting or were being fired as Stirling asserted his control.

Union critics look back on the 1980s and say Chavez didn't do enough to organize field workers, pointing out that Republican governors and presidents had not been able to stop the UFW's momentum in the past. But Dolores Huerta believes that the drastic change in politics in Sacramento and Washington, D.C., thwarted the union's traditional attempts to reach farmworkers. "People thought, well, Cesar should be running around the fields with a flag in his hand, right?" says Huerta, insistent that Chavez never abandoned field-level organizing. "People were unaware—because we got no press—that we didn't get the elections certified, and so people thought that Cesar wasn't organizing." Her claim of ongoing elections is backed by Stirling's own statistics, which show that, despite all the fighting over the farm-labor law and the reported turmoil within the UFW, there were still one hundred farmworker elections on California ranches in 1983. By the end of that year, the union still had 143 contracts in California as well as a number of pacts with growers in Florida and Texas.

While the number of workers covered by UFW contracts had fallen significantly from its 1980 peak, there was still enough strength to fund union operations, allowing Cesar to focus on expanding the UFW base. Chavez was developing plans to work with the Mexican government on an unprecedented offer of medical benefits to union members' families south of the border. He was also setting up a new membership plan that would allow farmworkers to be associated with the union even if they were not working under union contracts. Despite the problems, Chavez remained in high regard among farmworkers, who in 1983 told university researchers that they overwhelmingly viewed the UFW as their best avenue to get raises and to improve field conditions.

CHAPTER 4

THE LEGACY OF CESAR CHAVEZ

Union in Decline

Frank Bardacke

Frank Bardacke, author of the following selection, participated in many civil rights demonstrations and closely followed the farmworkers' movement. He attended Chavez's funeral and wrote a polemical assessment of the current condition of the UFW entitled: "Cesar's Ghost: Decline and Fall of the U.F.W." Bardacke charges that the failure of the union to mobilize and maintain "grassroots organizing" precipitated the dubious future of organized farm labor. Harvard graduate Frank Bardacke participated in the Student Nonviolence Coordinating Committee, and the 1960s Berkeley Free Speech movement. He currently teaches at the Watsonville Adult School.

Cesar, who was always good at symbols, saved his best for last: a simple pine box, fashioned by his brother's hands, carried unceremoniously through the Central Valley town he made famous. With some 35,000 people looking on.

Here was meaning enough, both for those who need it blunt and for those who like it subtle. No one—especially not the newspaper and TV reporters whose liberal sympathies had been one of his main assets—could fail to hear that pine box speak: Cesar Chavez's commitment to voluntary poverty extended even unto death. And perhaps a few among the crowd would get the deeper reference. Burial insurance had been Cesar's first organizing tool in building the National Farmworkers Association back in 1962. Many farmworkers, then and now, die so badly in debt that they can't afford to be buried. By joining up with Cesar and paying dues to the association, workers earned the right to take their final rest in a pine box, built by brother Richard.

The funeral march and picnic were near perfect. The friendly crowd was primarily Chicano, people who had driven a couple of hours up and over the Grapevine from Los Angeles to honor the man who was the authentic represen-

Frank Bardacke, "Cesar's Ghost: Decline and Fall of the U.F.W.," *The Nation*, July 26, 1993. Copyright © 1993 by The Nation, L.P. Reproduced by permission.

tative of their political coming of age in postwar America. Martin Luther King is the standard comparison, but Cesar Chavez was King and Jackie Robinson, too. Chicanos and Mexicans had played well in their own leagues—they built a lot of power in the railroad, mining and factory unions of the Southwest—but Cesar forced his way into the political big leagues, where Chicanos had always been excluded. And, like Robinson, he played on his own terms.

Not only Chicanos but all manner of farmworker supporters marched at the funeral: liberal politicians, celebrities, Catholic priests, grape and lettuce boycotters. This was fitting too, as Chavez had always insisted that his greatest contribution to the farmworker movement was the consumer boycott. The boycott, he argued, ended the debilitating isolation of farmworkers that had doomed their earlier organizing. And so it was right that the boycotters marched at Cesar's funeral, and it was their buttons (the word "grapes" or "uvas" with a ghostbuster line through it) that everyone wore.

What the march lacked was farmworkers, at least in mass numbers. Several buses had come down from the Salinas Valley, and farmworkers from the immediate area were well represented, but as a group, farmworkers added little weight to the funeral. I saw no banners from U.F.W. locals, nor did I see a single button or sign proclaiming the idea of farmworker power. And this, too, was symbolically perfect, for at the time of Cesar Chavez's death, the U.F.W. was not primarily a farmworker organization. It was a fundraising operation, run out of a deserted tuberculosis sanitarium in the Tehachapi Mountains, far from the fields of famous Delano, staffed by members of Cesar's extended family and using as its political capital Cesar's legend and the warm memories of millions of aging boycotters. . . .

So I was surprised by the farmworker presence at that first funeral march. Fewer than 200 people had shown up, but a good number of them were field workers. I ran into my old friend Roberto Fernandez, the man who taught me how to pack celery in the mid-seventies and who helped me make it on a piece-rate celery crew, where on good days we made over $15 an hour. . . .

Roberto, his 6-year-old daughter and I walked a short while on the march together, and when the other folks went into Asuncion Church to pray, the three of us walked back into town. I had seen Roberto off and on since I left our celery crew after the 1979 strike, but we had avoided discussing farmworker politics. Roberto is a committed Chavista and always could be counted on to give the official U.F.W. line. He was currently working on one of the few union contracts in town—not with the U.F.W. but with a rival independent union, as the U.F.W. no longer has any celery workers under contract. I asked him what went wrong in the fields.

"The Republicans replace the Democrats and ruined the law, and we no longer had any support in Sacramento."

"That's it? All the power we had, gone just because [Governor] Deukmejian replaced [Jerry] Brown?"

"The people were too ignorant."

"What do you mean?"

"We got swamped by people coming from small ranchos in Mexico who didn't know anything about unions. When the companies were letting our contracts expire and bringing in the labor contractors, we would go out to the people in the fields and try to explain to them about the union. But they didn't get it. They just wanted to work."

"I don't believe that. We had people from ranchos in Mexico on our U.F.W. crews. They were strong unionists; unions are not such a hard to understand."

"Well, Frank, you aren't ever going to believe that the workers were at fault, but I was there and I talked to them, and you weren't."...

MISSED OPPORTUNITIES

The virtual destruction of a unionized work force in the fields of California in the 1980s was due finally to the overwhelming social, financial and political power of the biggest business in our Golden State. The weight of the internal errors of the U.F.W. is secondary to the longstanding anti-union policies of the people who own and operate the most powerful agro-export industry in the world.

Nevertheless, in the late seventies, at the height of the U.F.W.'s strength among farmworkers, some in California agribusiness had come to the conclusion that Chavez's victory was inevitable and that they would have to learn to live with the U.F.W. Why wasn't the union—with perhaps 50,000 workers under contract and hundreds of militant activists among them—able to seize this historic opportunity?

The short answer is that within the U.F.W. the boycott tail

came to wag the farmworker dog. While it was not wrong of
Chavez to seek as much support as possible, this support
work, primarily the boycott, became the essential activity of
the union. Ultimately, it interfered with organizing in the
fields.

It was an easy mistake to fall into, especially as the failure
of the first grape strikes was followed so stunningly by the
success of the first grape boycott. The very best farmworker
activists, the strongest Chavistas, were removed from the
fields and direct contact with farmworkers, so that they
could be sent to work in the boycott offices of major cities.
From the point of view of building the boycott, it was a genius decision. But from the point of view of spreading the
union among farmworkers themselves, it was a disaster.

SHAME AND RESENTMENT

The manipulative use of farmworkers gave the union boycott
its texture and feel. In the mid-1970s a story circulated in
Salinas about a union meeting in the Imperial Valley called to
recruit workers to go to a press conference in Los Angeles to
support one of the boycotts. For the workers it meant a ten-
hour round-trip drive on one of their days off, but many of
them were willing to do it. These particular farmworkers
were mostly young piece-rate lettuce cutters who earned relatively high wages, and who, like a lot of working-class
people able to afford it, put their money into clothes and cars
which they sported on their days off. They were proud
people, volunteering to spend a weekend in Los Angeles organizing support for their movement. As the meeting closed,
Marshall Ganz—one of the union's top officials at the time—
had a final request. At the press conference everybody should
wear their work clothes.

The union officials didn't want farmworkers to appear as
regular working people appealing for solidarity. They had to
be poor and suffering, hats in hand, asking for charity. It
may have made a good press conference, but the people who
told the story were angered and shamed.

What the U.F.W. called publicity strikes hurt quite a bit
too. Typically, the union would enter a small spontaneous
walkout (a tactic California farmworkers have been using
for more than a hundred years to drive up wages at harvest
time), escalate local demands as a way of publicizing the
overall plight of farmworkers and then leave. This played

well enough in New York and Chicago, but made it more difficult for farmworkers to win these local battles.

The union's strategy after passage of California's Agricultural Relations Act in 1975 was similar. The union would aim to win as many certification elections as possible, thereby demonstrating to Governor Jerry Brown, allies in the California legislature, boycott supporters around the world and even agribusiness that it had the allegiance of a large majority of California farmworkers. The U.F.W. hoped that this would result in some sort of statewide master agreement, imposed from above, that would cover farmworkers in most of the larger agribusiness companies.

As with the publicity strikes, the U.F.W. came onto a ranch with its high-powered organizing techniques, explained how important it was for people to vote for the union, usually won the elections and then left. Less than a third of the elections resulted in union contracts, however; too many workers felt used and deserted; and opposition to the U.F.W. grew in the fields. . . .

It was the lack of strength among farmworkers that made the 1983 change in the Governor's office and the weakening of boycott support so devastating. Some of the biggest ranches reorganized their operations and replaced union contracts with labor contractors. Others let their U.F.W. contracts expire and refused to renegotiate them. In both cases, the union was powerless to stop them; the years of neglecting farmworker organizing finally took their toll. . . .

THE UNION FELL APART

I talked to one of the men, Aristeo Zambrano, a few weeks after the [Chavez] funeral. Aristeo was one of eleven children born to a farmworker family in Chavinda, Michoacan. His father worked as a bracero between 1945 and 1960, and after getting his papers fixed, he brought his son, then 14, to Hayward, California, in 1969. Aristeo moved to Salinas in 1974 and got a job cutting broccoli at a U.F.W.-organized company—Associated Produce. He was elected to the ranch committee in 1976; for the next six years he was an active unionist, re-elected to the committee every year and then to the position of paid representative, until he was fired by Chavez.

I asked him the same question I had asked Roberto Fernandez. What went wrong? How did the union fall so far so fast? . . .

"The problem developed way before we were fired in 1982. In the mid-seventies, when I became an activist, Chavez was making every decision in the union. . . . He was incapable of sharing power. So after the 1982 convention—the first U.F.W. convention that was not simply a staged show, the first convention where true disagreements came to the floor—he fired us. First he tried to organize recall elections, so that farmworkers would replace us. But he couldn't do it. We had too much support in the fields.

"We went back to the fields, and tried to continue organizing, but it was impossible. The damage had been done. People were scared or gave up on the union. They could see that the union did not belong to the workers, that it was Chavez's own personal business, and that he would run his business as he pleased. Farmworkers were good for boycotting, or walking the picket lines, or paying union dues, but not for leading our union. . . .

"Chavez built the union and then he destroyed it. The U.F.W. self-destructed. When the Republicans came back in the 1980s and the growers moved against the union, there wasn't any farmworker movement left."

What happens next? There was a feeling of optimism at the funeral. So many people together again, united by their respect for Chavez, pledging themselves to renewed effort. In her own fashion, Dolores Huerta, one of the founders of the union, expressed the hope of the crowd in her eulogy. "Cesar," she said, "died in peace, in good health, with a serene look on his face. It was as if he had chosen to die at this time . . . at this Easter time. . . . He died so that we would wake up. He died so that the union might live."

In the several weeks since the funeral, I have pondered Dolores's image of Chavez as the U.F.W.'s Christ, dying so that we might live. In one way, it is perfect. All the talk of [Saul] Alinsky and community organizing aside, Cesar Chavez was essentially a lay Catholic leader. His deepest origins were not in Alinsky's radical Community Service Organization but in the cursillos de Cristiandad movement, the intense encounters of Catholic lay people, first developed by the clergy in Franco's Spain and transplanted to the New World in the 1950s. The song they brought with them was "De Colores," and their ideology was a combination of anticommunism and personal commitment of ordinary lay people to the Gospel's version of social justice. Chavez, throughout his public life, remained true to that commitment. What many of the liberals and radicals on the staff of the union could never understand was that all the fasts, the long marches, the insistence on personal sacrifice and the flirting with sainthood were not only publicity gimmicks, they were the essential Chavez.

An Urban Icon

John Gregory Dunne

In 1971, long before Chavez's death, John Gregory
Dunne eulogized the labor leader in a controversial
article for the *Atlantic* magazine. Dunne predicted
the legacy of Chavez would be based more on a culti-
vated mystique than for any particular achievements.
He credits Chavez with germinating a cultural pride
in the economically depressed inner city barrios, but
is dubious about so-called successes in the vineyards
of Delano. Dunne believes media hype and political
grandstanding inflated the stature of a man who may
be in actuality more flash than substance. Novelist,
screenwriter, and journalist, Dunne is a frequent
contributor to the *New Yorker* magazine.

We have become a nation of ten-minute celebrities, pander-
ing to the cultural nymphomania of the media. People, issues, and causes hit the charts like rock groups, and with
approximately as much staying power. For all the wrong
reasons, Chavez had all the right credentials—mysticism,
nonviolence, the nobility of the soil—credentials that explained less about him than they did about the national lust
for glamour and image and promise. One could thus fete the
grape workers on a Long Island estate, as the rich and beau-
tiful once did, without a thought about the Suffolk County
potato workers only a few miles away living in conditions as
wretched as any picker's in California.

And so I followed the strike from afar until that day last
summer, when after five years of bitter struggle, it finally
came to an end. "We are happy peace has come to this valley," a growers' spokesman said at the contract-signing ceremony. "It has been a mutual victory."

"Mutual victory"—the phrase had the hollow sound of
rhetoric, and one thing I learned in Delano that summer of
1966 was that the territory behind rhetoric is too often

mined with equivocation. I wondered who, if anyone, was really victorious, wondered how ambiguity had tinctured victory. And so for the first time in four years, I returned to Delano, goaded there by the instinctive feeling that there are no solutions, only at best amelioration, and never ultimate answers, final truths.

MAN OF THE DISPOSSESSED

It was Robert Kennedy who legitimized Chavez. Prior to 1966, when the U.S. Senate Subcommittee on Migratory Labor held hearings in the valley, no Democrat would touch the Chavez movement. It had been necessary to attract a few Southern votes if prolabor legislation were to pass in the Congress, and Southern agrarians would not toss even a bone toward labor unless farm workers were excluded from all provisions of any proposed bill. Robert Kennedy was no stranger to either expedience or good politics, and, along with most of organized labor, saw little to be gained from an identification with Chavez. But he was persuaded to attend the hearings by one of his aides, Peter Edelman, acting in concert with a handful of union officials alive to the drama in Delano. Even flying to California, Kennedy was reluctant to get involved, demanding of his staff, "Why am I going?" He finally showed up at the hearings a day late. The effect was electric, a perfect meeting of complementary mystiques. Kennedy—arrogant, a predator in the corridors of power; and Chavez—nonviolent, Christian, mystical, not without a moral imperative of his own. The Kennedys sponged up ideas, and implicit in Chavez was the inexorable strength of an idea whose time had come. Kennedy's real concern for the farm workers helped soften his image as a self-serving keeper of his brother's flame and in turn plugged Chavez into the power outlets of Washington and New York. For the first time, Chavez became fashionable, a national figure registering on the nation's moral thermometer. Robert Kennedy and Cesar Chavez—the names seemed wired into the same circuitry, the one a spokesman, the other a symbol for the constituency of the dispossessed. . . .

The curious thing about Cesar Chavez is that he is as little understood by those who would canonize him as by those who would condemn him. To the saint-makers, Chavez seemed the perfect candidate. He had all the elements of the salable symbol—mysticism, nonviolence, the nobility of the

soil. His crusade was devoid of the ambiguities of urban conflict. With the farm workers there were no nagging worries
about the mugging down the block, the rape across the
street, the car boosted in front of the house. It was a cause
populated by simple Mexican peasants with noble agrarian
ideas, not by surly black ghetto unemployables with low IQ's
and Molotov cocktails.

All that is missing in this fancy is any apprehension of
where the real importance of Cesar Chavez lies. The saintly
virtues he had aplenty; it is doubtful that the media would
have been attracted to him were it not for those virtues, and
without the attention of the media the strike could not have
survived. But Chavez also had the virtues of the labor leader,
less applauded publicly, perhaps, but no less admirable in
the rough going—a will of iron, a certain deviousness, an
ability to hang tough in the clinches. Together these twin
disciplines kept what often seemed a hopeless struggle alive
for six years, six years that kindled an idea that made the
idealized nuances of Delano pale by comparison.

For the ultimate impact of Delano will be felt not so much
on the farm as in the city. In the vineyards Chavez fertilized
an ethnic and cultural pride ungerminated for generations,
but it was in the barrio that this new sense of racial identity
flourished as if in a hothouse. At one time four fifths of the
Mexican-American population lived in the rural outback,
but as the farm worker became a technological as well as a
social victim, his young deserted the hoe for the car wash.
Today that same four fifths float through the urban barrio
like travelers without passports, politically impoverished,
spiritually disenfranchised. State and municipal govern-
ments have so carefully charted the electoral maps that it is
impossible for a Mexican-American to get elected without
Anglo sufferance. California's only Mexican-American con-
gressman depends on Anglo suburbs for more than half his
support, and in the state legislature the gerrymandering is
even more effective; there was in 1971 only one Mexican as-
semblyman and no state senator. It was a system that placed
high premium on the Tio Taco, or Uncle Tom.

PRIDE AWAKENED

But since Delano, there is an impatience in the barrio with
old formulas and old deals and old alliances, a dissatisfac-
tion with a diet of crumbs, a mood—more than surly, though

not yet militant—undermining and finally beginning to crack the ghetto's historic inertia. Drive down Whittier Boulevard in East Los Angeles, a slum in the Southern California manner, street after street of tiny bungalows and parched lawns and old cars, a grid of monotony. The signs are unnoticed at first, catching the eye only after the second or third sighting, whitewashed on fences and abandoned storefronts, the paint splattered and uneven, signs painted on the run in the dark of night, *"Es mejor morir de pie que vivir de rodillas"*—"Better to die standing than live on your knees." The words are those of Emiliano Zapata, but the spirit that wrote them there was fired by Cesar Chavez.

The pride that Chavez helped awaken took on a different tone in the barrio from in the vineyards. The farm workers' movement was essentially nonviolent, an effort based on keeping and exhibiting the moral advantage. But in East Los Angeles today the tendency is to pick up life's lessons less from Gandhi than from the blacks. Traditionally, brown and black have been hostile, each grappling for that single spot on the bottom rung of the social ladder. To the Mexican-American the Anglo world held out the bangle of assimilation, a bribe to the few that kept the many docile. Denied to blacks, assimilation for years robbed the Chicano community of a nucleus of leadership. Today the forfeiture of this newly acquired cultural awareness seems to the young Chicano a prohibitive price to pay. The new courses in social bribery are taught by the blacks.

REBELLION OF THE DISPOSSESSED

The barrio is learning from the blacks the political sex appeal of violence. Three times in the past year East Los Angeles has erupted. The body count is still low, less than the fingers on one hand, hardly enough to merit a headline outside Los Angeles County. The official riposte is a call for more law and order. The charges of police brutality clash with the accusations of outside agitation. But beyond the rhetoric there is new attention focused on the ghetto. The vocabulary of the dispossessed is threat and riot, the Esperanto of a crisis-reacting society, italicizing the poverty and discrimination and social deprivation in a way that no funded study or government commission ever could.

Like Malcolm X and Martin Luther King, Cesar Chavez stands astride history less for what he accomplished than for what he is. Like them he has forged "in the smithy of his soul," as Joyce said, the creative consciousness of a people. He is the manifestation of *la raza,* less the saint his admirers make him out to be than a moral obsessive, drilling into the decay of a system that has become a mortuary of hopes.

An Inspirational Hero

Charles J. Ogletree Jr.

Cesar Chavez's message that justice can be achieved through dignity resonated with the author of this 1994 article, a lawyer who attributes the shaping of his legal methods to the "rebellious influence of Chavez." Charles J. Ogletree Jr. cites Chavez as an inspiration to oppressed people of all backgrounds, and lauds the perseverance demonstrated by Chavez throughout his forty year campaign to aid the downtrodden. He compares Chavez with Gandhi and Martin Luther King Jr., but ultimately argues that history will recognize Chavez in his own right. Charles J. Ogletree Jr. is a Harvard Law School professor and trustee of the University of the District of Columbia.

In April 1993, we lost a man whom United States Senator Robert F. Kennedy once described as "one of the heroic figures of our time." César Chávez, considered by one Chicano leader as "the principle figure in the Chicano civil rights awakening," is the man who organized and led the United Farm Workers ("UFW") in its struggle against some of the largest and most powerful growers in the country. Perhaps the UFW's best known effort was the international boycott of Delano table grapes, the UFW thunderbird seals on grape crates in supermarkets today testify to Chávez' perserverance and eventual victory in that battle.

However, César Chávez did much more than lead a few boycotts and rattle some large corporations. He gave voices to the before-silent and unseen Chicano farm workers in Southern California making the group part of the wider worldwide movement known as *La Causa*. Partly through Chávez' efforts, the unique history and culture of Mexican-Americans gained national attention and became that which the dominant society has since enveloped as distinctly "American."

Chávez, for Chicanos and all Latinos, was more than just

Charles J. Ogletree Jr., "The Quiet Storm: The Rebellious Influence of Cesar Chavez," *Harvard Latino Law Review*, Fall 1994. Copyright © 1994 by Charles J. Ogletree Jr. Reproduced by permission of the publisher.

an activist, organizer, and supporter of culture. He was, as California state senator Art Torres said at the time of Chávez' death, "our Gandhi. . . . [O]ur Dr. Martin Luther King." In his vision for the UFW, Chávez realized that his efforts went far beyond the California fields and picket lines. He once noted that:

> regardless of what the future holds for our union, regardless of what the future holds for farm workers, our accomplishments cannot be undone. The consciousness and pride that were raised by our union are alive and thriving inside millions of young Hispanics who will never work on a farm.

JUSTICE THROUGH DIGNITY

Chávez is more than a Chicano Gandhi or King; he is an inspiration in his own right. Chávez' involvement with *La Causa* symbolized "that individuals can make a difference, can help themselves and others, and can keep their principles, although the task is hard and is never-ending." Thus, another name is added to the list of individuals who have inspired a group of people to seek reform while adhering to the basic principles of humanity and dignity.

Sadly enough, Chávez and the UFW lost influence over the past decade; at times, it appeared that the movement's few appearances in the mainstream press centered only around the legal and internal problems of the union. Nonetheless, Chávez' message of justice through dignity never dimmed; rather it continues to apply, even after his death, to oppressed people everywhere. . . .

[T]he value of César Chávez' message has not diminished. For three decades he inspired thousands to sacrifice and stand up for justice and human dignity by fasting along with Chávez, joining picket lines, choosing to pay decent wages, or simply refusing to buy Delano grapes or other boycotted products. He remains a symbol of empowerment and pride, not only for Chicanos or for workers, but for all people who are oppressed and exploited, as well as for any who pause to help them. . . .

INFLUENCE OF KING AND GANDHI

In organizing the UFW and in putting the union's cohesion to work for *La Causa*, Chávez learned from the precedents of Martin Luther King, Jr. and Mahatma Gandhi; it should be no surprise then, that Chávez' methods for creating mass

movements on behalf of social justice resembled those of
these two leaders. More specifically, Chávez was able to organize the farm workers and to bring others to support their
cause through three mobilizing techniques used by Gandhi
and King: the generation of pride in a group identity; the
mobilization of religious feeling on behalf of a policy and
practice of nonviolence; and the use of personal and visible
self-sacrifice. . . .

Like King, Chávez emphasized the transcendental, group-
defining nature of the struggle in which his group engaged.
The agricultural workers' campaigns and strikes represented their demands that they be given the basic rights afforded other groups in society—rights which in effect de-
fined those other groups' members as citizens with publicly,
legally recognized worth. The very name *La Causa* called attention to the universality of Chávez' movement's ultimate
goals: the UFW and its component organizations worked not
for a specific cause, but for "the cause" of human dignity, a
dignity which their group deserved and which other groups
had already received. . . .

Mahatma Gandhi, who led India's movement to rid itself of
British colonial rule, believed that non-violence presented
the only moral means of sustaining an organized protest
movement. In forcing the wrongdoer to see the concrete
effects his evil had on others, Gandhi's practice of non-
resistance caused the wrongdoer to notice the non-resister as
a human being, promoting a sense of community and brotherhood. Non-violence also had other tactical uses: it ensured
that the greater community outside the group would view the
group's actions sympathetically, creating further momentum
for change. Gandhi emphasized the dignity of man and the
interrelatedness of the community as a tool for organizing
and motivating change. A man with dignity not only con-
founded aggression, but shamed his attacker as well. . . .

Chávez interpreted the non-violent ethic at its most fundamental to mean "that masses of people come to the aid of
their less fortunate brothers who are legally, legitimately,
and nonviolently trying to get a better life for themselves and
their families." While not solely a religious sentiment, this
kind of empathy and brotherhood is at the heart of Christian
teachings and had a powerful influence on his ability to organize and raise support for *La Causa.*

Chávez not only demonstrated how his cause grew out of

the moral universals which he derived from Christianity; he also relied directly on religious teachings and symbols to help spread his message. . . .

INTERCONNECTED STRUGGLES

Chávez always recognized that the struggle for civil and human rights went beyond the calls of migrant farm workers in California. He was able to see the connections and the similarities among the struggles of Latinos, Blacks, Jews, and other minorities. When students at the University of California at Los Angeles Law School protested the school's lack of progress in admitting minority students and in hiring minority faculty, César Chávez was one of the first to come forward and provide support. In a rally held on the UCLA campus, Chávez expressed his unequivocal support for students and acknowledged how important their role had been in

---

HOLIDAY HONORS CHAVEZ

On August 18, 2000, Gray Davis, the governor of California, signed legislation that declared March 30 "Cesar Chavez Day." As a result, Cesar Chavez became the first Hispanic ever to be recognized with a paid state holiday. Reporter Rich Heffern describes the creation of the new holiday.

Once again California, first in freeways and orange groves, leads the nation—this time in honoring the life of the country's foremost Hispanic civil rights leader with a state holiday. State employees will get a paid day off this year, on Friday, March 30, in honor of Cesar Chavez, leader of the United Farm Workers union. Legislation creating a holiday on the Monday or Friday nearest his March 31 birthday was approved by the California legislature and signed by Gov. Gray Davis last summer.

"When children learn about the great life of Martin Luther King, Jr., they will also learn about the great life of Cesar Chavez," said Davis when he signed the California legislation on Aug. 18, 2000. "With an unconquerable spirit and undeniable cause, Chavez led a labor movement which set into motion such powerful, sweeping changes that the impact is still being felt today."

The law creates what is described as the nation's first paid state holiday honoring a Latino or a labor union figure. . . .

According to new state guidelines, California schools will have the option of commemorating Chavez with a "Day of Service and Learning." At participating schools, a state-funded

supporting farm workers. Chávez observed:

> Who are we fighting for today to come into this university? What is the fight all about? It's about working class families, and the kids who come from working class families, in many cases very much exploited, who don't have the money to be able to have the things that creates an education. Working class students come here because we are exploited in the fields and in the factories, because we don't have the money to attend the private schools, because our parents work for peanuts for a day in the fields or a day in the factories. That's what produces the student that we're now fighting for, to make sure that he's admitted, that she's admitted here in this university.
>
> If we have anything going for us, it is the student who is here, the minority student, the Chicano student here today, who is advocating for the one who will come tomorrow.

Chávez' support for students, in turn, led to student sup-

---

curriculum will be used in the morning to teach students about Chavez and the history of the farm labor movement in the United States. In the afternoon, students will perform community service.

"We wanted to be able to provide young people knowledge about Cesar Chavez, who he was, what his philosophy was, but also a way to practice it," said United Farm Workers president, Arturo Rodriguez, who pushed for the educational component as a way to keep the Chavez legacy alive.

After much debate, California Democrats unanimously supported the legislation, which was initiated by Sen. Richard Polanco, a Los Angeles Democrat. Many Republicans, primarily from the Central Valley where Chavez is still a controversial figure, voted against it or didn't vote at all. Opponents criticized the cost of the holiday. . . .

Oakland mayor and former governor Jerry Brown said Chavez was "the most important labor leader since World War II." U.S. Sen. Edward Kennedy, D-Mass., called him "one of the great pioneers for civil rights and human rights of our century."

"He was a common man who did uncommon things," said Rodriguez. "Even people who weren't around when Cesar Chavez was alive will recognize now what he did. To have someone in our ethnic group recognized like this, it brings us a lot of pride."

Rich Heffern, *National Catholic Reporter*, March 2001.

port for his struggle then and even now; his example proved
central to the success of a recent hunger strike on the UCLA
campus. Indeed, Chávez was one of the figures who most influenced my decision to consider a career in public service,
and more particularly a career as a public defender. The
emotional commitments which underlay his efforts on behalf of farm workers resemble the motivations which led me
to represent indigents in the criminal justice system. . . .

TESTIMONIAL

At first I knew César Chávez only as "The Mexican Organizer." In my early teens, I was uninformed about Chávez'
goals. In fact, most of the news I heard painted César Chávez
as an annoyance rather than as a positive contributor to life
in the Valley. This misleading "news" originated, in large
part, from the efforts of farmers to destroy the movement
that Chávez was building. As time went on, I began to recognize the magnitude of César Chávez' efforts and the positive impact those efforts were having on all workers in the
San Joaquín Valley. When he complained about the lettuce
and about the poor wages that farmworkers received, it was
an indication of how agricultural workers were subjected to
inhumane conditions for no good reason. When he gave us
information about pesticides and the harm that they could
cause to individuals and their families, it was graphic evidence of the insensitivity of the growers.

I was also beginning to recognize that Chávez' ultimate
impact would extend far beyond California. I had read about
Dr. Martin Luther King, Jr. and had witnessed the impact he
had in galvanizing African-Americans to oppose segregation. I had read about Mahatma Gandhi and had been impressed with his ability to capture the spirit of millions of In-
dians and engage in effective civil disobedience. I also knew
that both of these leaders had engaged in self-sacrifice for
the betterment of their peoples.

But I had the opportunity to watch César Chávez' work in
a very personal way. I did not read about his organizing in
the newspaper or watch it on television, but actively participated in the events. I participated in rallies in such places as
Delano, Salinas, Fresno, and Bakersfield. In each of these in-
stances I felt like I was part of the movement. Even though I
had thought of César Chávez' work as focused on Mexican
farm workers, it became clear to me that he was trying to

create opportunities for all. I saw that his appeal was broad, universal, and effective. When we marched in Delano to complain about lettuce, it was a unified effort to challenge prevailing notions and power relationships. When he called for the boycott of grapes and we saw the UFW label on products, we knew that we were having an impact.

For the first time, these marches gave me a sense of what a multicultural world would look like. There we were, black, brown, and white, young and old, Republican and Democrat, conservative and liberal, wealthy and poor, marching in the cause of justice. It was the kind of spirited and enthusiastic show of unity that ultimately influenced my decision to use my legal talents in aid of less advantaged groups in this country. . . .

A QUIET STORM OF REBELLION

Despite the powerful level of moral commitment that Chávez expressed on behalf of farm workers, he unfortunately did not receive the kind of national support that was given to other organizers. It should also be noted that Chávez did not seek any notoriety; he was quite content focusing on the success of *La Causa* rather than reading press clippings or focusing on self-promotion. While the history books are full of references to Mahatma Gandhi, Malcolm X, and Martin Luther King, Jr., most children, except in California, have little knowledge of the commitment of César Chávez to the struggle for civil and human rights.

This is an unfortunate fact of our society and one that warrants careful attention by scholars. Perhaps César Chávez has been comparatively overlooked by the larger culture because the injustices he addressed are wrongly viewed as local or regional; perhaps broad ignorance of Chávez' accomplishments can be traced to a widespread desire to ignore the continuing problems faced by the groups he represented. Whatever the reason, Chávez' enormous record of accomplishments should not go unnoticed because of his untimely death. It is of critical importance that those who have been touched by him recount those stories, and memorialize his broad impact on progressive politics and human rights.

Since César Chávez was so critical to the success of the struggle for workers rights in the 1950s, 1960s, and 1970s, it is incumbent on those who believe in his ideas and the principles he espoused to write the articles and give the speeches that bear witness to his many accomplishments as a great advocate for the poor. . . .

There is no doubt in my mind that my early vision, judgment, and commitment to the cause of the unrepresented was due in a large part to attendance at those early rallies, boycotts, and strategy sessions organized by César Chávez and the United Farm Workers Union. We owe him a great debt of gratitude for beginning the small storm that ultimately has led to a wide level of consciousness among workers about their rights. It is in his memory and pursuant to his legacy that we must continue the storm.

The Hope of a New Humanity

Richard Griswold del Castillo and Richard A. Garcia

Richard Griswold del Castillo and Richard A. Garcia were two among thousands of mourners who marched in the funeral procession of Cesar Chavez. Reflecting on the event and on Chavez's life, the authors acknowledge the impact Chavez had upon the labor movement and the lives of Hispanics in general. But perhaps more significantly, del Castillo and Garcia attest that Chavez's dedication to the rights of the poor and oppressed set examples of justice and humanity for all to follow.

Richard Griswold del Castillo is Professor of Mexican American Studies at San Diego State University, and Richard A. Garcia is a professor of History at California State University, Hayward.

In the early 1990s, César Chávez continued his fight for the farm workers. It was a period of tremendous struggle and sacrifice. Journalists and op-ed writers occasionally devoted space to the problems the union faced, and the media's mood was largely pessimistic, if not critical. Essayists again blamed the declining fortunes of the UFW on the contradictory nature of César's leadership. His advocacy of democracy in union organization was contrasted with the increasing role of the Chávez family in top positions. Another anomaly seemed to be his trust in volunteer workers alongside his efforts to professionalize the union's administration. His loyalty to old friends and allies was undermined by bitter attacks by liberal journalists—enthusiastic supporters from the 1970s—who now were more critical. They reported internal dissent in the union. These criticisms hurt Chávez and forced him to draw to him a tight circle of loyalists.

The union was also beset with serious financial problems, arising from lawsuits. In 1991, the 4th District Court in

California upheld an earlier judgment against the UFW, in favor of Daggio Inc., an Imperial Valley grower, for $1.7 million (and including interest, the final cost to the union could exceed $2.4 million). The award arose out of a 1979 strike by vegetable workers that resulted in property damage and the death of striker Rufino Contreras. To pay the fine, the UFW mounted a nationwide direct-mail campaign. But almost immediately another lawsuit threatened the UFW's existence, this one by Bruce Church Inc., who won a $5.4 million judgment for damages alleged to have been incurred during the boycott. The union appealed and is still waiting for a final resolution.

Chávez continued to appear at fund-raising rallies at college and university campuses and traveled to promote the grape boycott. He also stepped up organizing in the fields. Ranch by ranch and week by week during the summer and fall of 1992, César and the UFW staff sought to advance the union's issues. He continued organizing the grape boycott to force growers to sign contracts controlling pesticide use. In 1992, the union helped organize large-scale walkouts in the Coachella Valley during the summer grape harvest, protesting a lack of drinking water and sanitary facilities. They won concessions from the grower, allowing a workers' committee to watchdog the situation. Also in 1992, in the San Joaquin Valley, Chávez organized walkouts and protests; and in the Salinas Valley, more than ten thousand farm workers, led by Chávez, staged a protest march in support of better conditions in the fields.

Up to his death, Chávez remained confident about the ultimate success of the UFW. In late April 1993 he traveled to San Luis, Arizona (near his birthplace), to testify in the union's appeal against the $5.4 million award to Bruce Church Inc. Chávez stayed with a farm worker family and early in the week began a fast to gain moral strength. On Thursday his friends convinced him to break his fast and he went to sleep, apparently exhausted. That night, he died in his sleep.

THOUSANDS MOURN CHÁVEZ

The unexpected death of Chávez on 23 April 1993 was a major shock to his supporters throughout the world. The outpouring of condolences that followed was testimony to his importance: he was a leader who had touched the conscience of

America. In addition to President Clinton's "authentic hero" proclamation, Art Torres, a state senator, for example, called him "our Ghandi" and "our Dr. Martin Luther King." Lane Kirkland, president of the AFL-CIO, said that "the improved lives of millions of farm workers and their families will endure as a testimonial to César and his life's work."

Field workers, too, offered eulogies: Manuel Amaya said: "God has taken the strongest arm that we have, but we will continue." Remigio Gutiérrez said: "For all the workers, César was strong." But César himself had perhaps given the best eulogy, nine years earlier. Speaking before the Commonwealth Club of San Francisco, in 1984, he said: "Regardless of what the future holds for our union, regardless of what the future holds for farm workers, our accomplishments cannot be undone. The consciousness and pride that were raised by our union are alive and thriving inside millions of young Hispanics who will never work on a farm."

On the day of the funeral—Thursday, 29 April—more than 35,000 people followed the casket for three miles, from downtown Delano to the union's old headquarters at Forty Acres. They came from Toronto, Miami, Mexico . . . but mostly from California, where Chávez had worked most of his life. Parents took their children out of school and drove all night to give them the experience of participating in the funeral of a great leader of the poor. Middle-class Chicanos, taking time from work, marched—some perhaps for the first time—under a UFW flag. Cardinal Roger Mahony, who had worked as a mediator for the UFW more than twenty years earlier, led the huge outdoor mass, offering a personal condolence from the pope. César's twenty-seven grandchildren went up to the altar to lay on it a carving of a UFW eagle and a short-handled hoe. Dolores Huerta delivered the eulogy for the man she had worked with for more than forty years. Luis Valdez and the Teatro Campesino paid the final tribute. "You shall never die," said Valdez, "The seed of your heart will keep on singing, keep on flowering, for the cause."

LEGACY OF STRUGGLE

Not often does it occur that one must consciously participate in a historical event. [We] did so, that Thursday, with the thousands marching in Delano in honor of the memory of César Chávez. We were not quite sure what to expect, but we knew that we had to go.

We both had met and supported Chávez and the union in the late 1960s. Consequently, personal memories, personal reflections, and the fact that we had just finished jointly writing a biography of Chávez drove us—willingly—to pay our last respects. We certainly knew that many people would be there, but we were not prepared for the 35,000 and more that marched and went to the requiem mass.

Many were there to remember personal or public experiences of Chávez; many to experience "the end of an era." Some were there to liberate, to resurrect César Chávez from being merely a union leader, a Mexican-American hero, or a Chicano symbol. Many had already started to see him as a national metaphor of justice, humanity, equality, and freedom. It seemed that many of us were there, consciously or not, to place César Chávez in the pantheon of national and international American heroes—a tribute underscored by the statements sent by the pope, the president of Mexico, and President Clinton.

Most of the marchers were farm workers and their families: they had been touched by Chávez's presence. Also, many old students, old activists, now turned academics and intellectuals, were there to feel the innocence of the sixties, the fieriness of yesteryear's rebellion, the *lumbre* of Chávez's heart and will. We wanted that period back. Some of us had with us our children, hoping to give them an experience of continuity with our past.

The farm workers on the march felt Chávez in their hearts. We, the professors, felt him also in our heads—we were there to interpret. We were there along with the Chicano artists Montoya, Olmos, Alurista and others: in part to recall the romance that we once had with Chávez. However, if we could not feel it, we could at least write about it, or teach it. For us all, Chávez was the soul we had partly lost, not necessarily our ethnic one, nor our political one, but our human soul. Chávez, throughout his more than thirty years of organizing, never lost his spirit; he never became totally partisan in his politics. He believed in everyone—regardless of race or color. For Chávez, everyone was equal and deserved respect, dignity, and love.

LEGACY OF HOPE

Chávez always believed the words that thousands chanted on the march: *Se puede; si se puede*—It can be done, yes it can be done. Marching, we remembered Chávez's determination and constant hope; his deep belief that people can accomplish the impossible with cooperation, and God's help, as well as with hard work. Before Jesse Jackson said "Keep hope alive," Chávez had urged it. Before Jackson called for a Rainbow Coalition, Chávez had formed one. Before the Kennedys discovered the liberal mystique of the poor and poverty, Chávez had lived it and embraced it. And there they were—the Kennedy clan. Jesse Jackson, Willie Brown, Ron Dellums, Jerry Brown, Edward James Olmos, Jimmy Smits, Cheech Marin, Paul Rodriguez, Luis Valdez, the members of El Teatro Campesino, the Culture Clash comedy group, Martin Sheen, a remnant of the Brown Berets, and many other artists, politicians, and public figures. It was, in many ways, the sixties revisited. We felt the past being remade, the present suspended, and the future reenergized. It was a funeral, but it was more: it was a celebration of humanity and hope, a resurrection of Chávez's spirit: a *día de los Santos*, and a *día de los Muertos*.

For some, especially young people, it was a march of awareness, a day of learning and understanding, a forming of a new consciousness. We envied the fresh eyes from which they saw the march, the mass, the crowds, the waving flags, the priests, the politicians, the artists, and the farm workers. It was the young who, because of their perspective, allowed us to see beyond the chaos, hopelessness, and fragmentation of post-modern America. For a brief moment of time—that Thursday in 1993—on a hot day in Delano, we experienced the struggle, the life, and the tensions that Chávez had experienced: marching in the heat, thirsty, hungry, and sleepy. It was a renewal of community: we remembered; youth recognized. Briefly in Delano that hot day, we were all campesinos. We were one with César Chávez. We were part of the land, the struggle, and Chávez's hope that humanity would survive.

Together, we knew that as long as there were people like these young Chicanos/Latinos—and people who are observant, caring, romantic, and knowledgeable about the character, cause, and meaning of Chávez—there will be hope. Chávez the activist, alive and struggling in the 1960s, we once thought was only for us: the Chicanos, the Mexican Americans, the *Americans*, the radicals, the liberals, the innocent, the romantic—the ones who cared and were striving for a more just and equitable society. But now, in death, Chávez could be for everyone—all the new Hispanic and American generations of the 1990s and beyond, the generations of the twenty-first century. He could be a guiding mentor like Dr. Martin Luther King Jr. or John F. Kennedy. In a world in need of heroes, he (and people like Dolores Huerta) could be remembered for justice, freedom, and the hope of a new humanity. Chávez said almost thirty years ago:

> I am convinced that the truest act of courage, the strongest act of humanity, is to sacrifice ourselves for others in a totally non-violent struggle for justice . . . to be human is to suffer for others. . . . God help us to be human.

APPENDIX OF DOCUMENTS

DOCUMENT 1: A MISSION STATEMENT

Cesar Chavez issued this brief statement on December 15, 1964, a time when the National Farm Workers Association (NFWA) was building membership under Chavez's direction. He addresses his philosophy of leadership and stresses the importance of unity and sacrifice.

The mission of the leaders—which is the mission of any authority—is to sustain the movement, to keep the farm workers association on its destined path, to do what always has to be done so that the goals of the association can be reached.

If we want the movement to develop and the association to perfect itself, it is necessary to maintain a unity of doctrine, a unity of methods, and a unity of structure which will assure the goals of the movement.

This unity means that we must make sacrifices, but these are necessary to sustain the life of the whole organization; they are essential. When we decide on the goal of a particular work, it is necessary to hold on to it, not only with our lips, but always actively; it is necessary for this goal to become a role of life. He who *knows* principles is not equal to he who *loves* them.

Viva La Causa!

Winthrop Yinger, *Cesar Chavez: The Rhetoric of Nonviolence.* New York: Exposition Press, 1975.

DOCUMENT 2: THE FBI WATCHES CESAR CHAVEZ

In this excerpt from the FBI file on Cesar Chavez and the United Farm Workers, agents gather basic information on Chavez and his businesses and associates. Toward the end, an unnamed informant talks about NFWA membership and questions Chavez's motivation: He speculates that Chavez may be looking for personal monetary gain rather than the betterment of NFWA members.

CESAR E. CHAVEZ, a male Mexican, born 1/31/27, possibly at Delano, 5/3", 135 pounds, straight black hair, brown eyes, dark complexion, is the founder and Director of NFWA, with headquarters at 102 Albany Street, Delano, telephone number 8661.

CHAVEZ resides at 1221 Kensington Street, Delano, and also can be contacted at his brother's home, RICHARD CHAVEZ, a building inspector in Tulare County, California, who resides at 630 Belmont, Delano, telephone number 3036. The NFWA is active in Delano and Tulare County, but he has no idea of their membership total.

CHAVEZ spent about 14 years in San Jose, California, prior to 1963, as a recruiter for the Community Service Organization (CSO) at San Jose. CSO is a "war on poverty" type organization. Prior to his 14 years with CSO, CHAVEZ was with the same organization in Los Angeles and San Diego, California. Since January, 1963, CHAVEZ has resided in Delano.

CHAVEZ refuses to answer any questionnaires directed to him by Credit Bureaus or similar organizations. He has openly been called a Communist at Delano City Council meetings; however, [name deleted] does not possess any definite information in this regard. He does believe that CHAVEZ associates with "left wing" type individuals and is known to distribute the "People's World" from his office at Delano, free of charge. CHAVEZ publishes and sells a paper called "El Malcriado," described as the voice of the farm worker, and the official voice of the NFWA. . . .

CHAVEZ has publicly stated that his intention is to boycott downtown Delano businesses and have all Mexican-Americans buy through a NFWA store. At the present time, CHAVEZ sells automobile tires at the NFWA location at 102 Albany Street, Delano. . . .

NFWA is lead by CHAVEZ, and the purpose of this organization is suppossedly to improve the wages and living conditions of the migrant farm worker in Kern and Tulare Counties. NFWA claims they are an independent organization with offices at 102 Albany Street, Delano. [Informant] has no idea of the total membership of this organization. CHAVEZ rents the building at 102 Albany and also sells automobile tires and oil under the name Farm Workers Co-op, at this address. CHAVEZ has recently been cited for not having a business license, and is due to appear in the Delano Justice Court in the near future to show cause why he should not be penalized for operating a business without having a city license.

CHAVEZ has reportedly stated that he desires to open general stores in the San Joaquin Valley to sell "all commodities" to farm workers at discount prices and to, therefore, create a boycott of local businesses. At this point, CHAVEZ has only the tire and oil store mentioned above. CHAVEZ has also mentioned starting a Credit Union for farm workers who are members of the NFWA, however, he could furnish no additional information concerning this Credit Union or concerning the NFWA.

[Informant's] opinion is that CHAVEZ is not altogether sincere in his desire to assist migrant workers, but is solely interested in making a name for himself and to gain financially. The $267,887.00 grant approved by OEO for NFWA by the Federal Government has aroused considerable public opinion against making such a grant. His opinion is that CHAVEZ is not qualified to manage this large a sum. He has heard that CHAVEZ has only a grammar school education.

FBI file on Cesar Chavez and the United Farm Workers [microform]. Wilmington, DE: Scholarly Resources, 1996.

DOCUMENT 3: NFWA JOINS THE STRIKE

In this article written for the newsletter El Malcriado, *Chavez appeals for support, outlines the progressive events leading up to the strike, and describes the growing momentum of* La Causa *(The Cause).*

In a 400 square mile area halfway between Selma and Weedpatch, California, a general strike of farm workers has been going on for six weeks. The Filipinos, under AWOC AFL-CIO began the strike for a $1.40 per hour guarantee and a union contract. They were joined by the independent Farm Workers Association which has a membership of several thousand Mexican-Americans.

Filipino, Mexican-American and Puerto Rican workers have been manning picket lines daily for 41 days in a totally non-violent manner. Ranchers in the area, which include DiGiorgio Fruit, Schenley, and many independent growers, did not take the strike seriously at first. By the second or third week, however, they began taking another look—and striking back. Mechanized agriculture began picketing the pickets—spraying them with sulfur, running tractors by them to create dust storms, building barricades of farm machinery so that scabs could not see the pickets. These actions not only increased the determination of the strikers, but convinced some of the scabs that the ranchers were, in fact, less than human. Scabs quit work and the strike grew.

The growers hired security guards for $43 a day. They began driving their Thunderbirds, equipped with police dogs and rifles, up and down the roads. The people made more picket signs, drew in their belts, and kept marching.

Production was down 30% and the growers began looking for more and more scabs. They went to Fresno and Bakersfield and Los Angeles to find them. They didn't tell the workers that they would be scab crews. The pickets followed them into every town and formed ad hoc strike committees to prevent scabbing. They succeeded in these towns. Within two weeks, only one bus, with half a dozen winos, escorted by a pearl gray Cadillac, drove into the strike zone. A new plan was formed. The ranchers would advertise in South Texas and old Mexico. They bring these workers in buses and the workers are held in debt to the rancher before they even arrive in town. We have a new and more difficult task ahead of us with these scabs.

As our strike has grown, workers have matured and now know why and how to fight for their rights. As the strike has grown into a movement for justice by the lowest paid workers in America, friends of farm workers have begun to rally in support of LA CAUSA. Civil rights, church, student and union groups help with food and money.

We believe that this is the beginning of a significant drive to achieve equal rights for agricultural workers. In order to enlist your full support and to explain our work to you, I would like to bring some of our pickets and meet with you.

VIVA LA CAUSA Y
VIVA LA HUELGA
Cesar Estrada Chavez
General Director,
National Farm Workers Association

Cesar Chavez, "We Shall Overcome," *El Malcriado,* September 16, 1965.

DOCUMENT 4: THE PLAN OF DELANO

Cesar Chavez integrated cultural traditions into his leadership methodology. He continued a Mexican tradition on the occasion of the Delano to Sacramento pilgrimage in 1966 when he first issued this proclamation, "The Plan of Delano." The plan outlines the propositions and goals of a farmworker "revolution."

Plan for the liberation of the Farm Workers associated with the Delano Grape Strike in the State of California, seeking social justice in farm labor with those reforms that they believe necessary for their well-being as workers in these United States.

We the undersigned, gathered in Pilgrimage to the capital of the State in Sacramento in penance for all the failings of Farm Workers, as free and sovereign men, do solemnly declare before the civilized world which judges our actions, and before the nation to which we belong, the propositions we have formulated to end the injustice that oppresses us.

We are conscious of the historical significance of our Pilgrimage. It is clearly evident that our path travels through a valley well known to all Mexican farm workers. We know all of these towns of Delano, Madera, Fresno, Modesto, Stockton and Sacramento, because along this very same road, in this very same valley, the Mexican race has sacrificed itself for the last hundred years. Our sweat and our blood have fallen on this land to make other men rich. This Pilgrimage is a witness to the suffering we have seen for generations.

The Penance we accept symbolizes the suffering we shall have in order to bring justice to these same towns, to this same valley. The Pilgrimage we make symbolizes the long historical road we have traveled in this valley alone, and the long road we have yet to travel, with much penance, in order to bring about the Revolution we need, and for which we present the propositions in the following plan:

1. This is the beginning of a social movement in fact and not in pronouncements. We seek our basic, God-given rights as human beings. Because we have suffered—and are not afraid to suffer—in order to survive. We are ready to give up everything, even our lives in our fight for social justice. We shall do it without violence because that is our destiny. . . .

2. We seek the support of all political groups and protection of the government, which is also our government, in our struggle. For too many years we have been treated like the lowest of the low. Our wages and working conditions have been determined from above, because irresponsible legislators who could have helped us, have supported the rancher's argument that the plight of the farm worker was a "special case." They saw the obvious effects of an unjust system, starvation wages, contractors, day hauls, forced migration, sickness, illiteracy, camps and sub-human living conditions, and acted as if they were irremediable causes. The farm worker has been abandoned to his own fate—without representation, without power—subject to mercy and caprice of the rancher. We are tired of words, of betrayals, of indifference. To the politicians we say that the years are gone when the farm worker said nothing and did nothing to help himself. From this movement shall spring leaders who shall understand us, lead us, be faithful to us, and we shall elect them to represent us. WE SHALL BE HEARD.

3. We seek, and have, the support of the Church in what we do. At the head of the Pilgrimage we carry LA VIRGEN DE LA GUADALUPE (the Virgin of Guadalupe) because she is ours, all ours, Patroness of the Mexican people. We also carry the Sacred Cross and the Star of David because we are not sectarians, and because we ask the help and prayers of all religions. All men are brothers—sons of the same God; that is why we say to all men of good will, in the words of Pope Leo XIII, "Everyone's first duty is to protect the workers from the greed of speculators who use human beings as instruments to provide themselves with money. It is neither just nor human to oppress men with excessive work to the point where their minds become enfeebled and their bodies worn out." GOD SHALL NOT ABANDON US.

4. We are suffering. We have suffered, and we are not afraid to suffer in order to win our cause. We have suffered unnumbered ills and, crimes in the name of the law of the land. Our

men, women, and children have suffered not only the basic brutality of stoop labor, and the most obvious injustices of the system; they have also suffered the desperation of knowing that that system caters to the greed of callous men and not to our needs. Now we will suffer for the purpose of ending the poverty, the misery, and the injustice, with the hope that our children will not be exploited as we have been. They have imposed hungers on us, and now we hunger for justice. We draw our strength from the very despair in which we have been forced to live. WE SHALL ENDURE.

5. We shall unite. We have learned the meaning of UNITY. We know why these United States are just that—united. The strength of the poor is also in union. We know that the poverty of the Mexican or Filipino worker in California is the same as that of all farm workers across the country, the Negroes and poor whites, the Puerto Ricans, Japanese, and Arabians; in short, all of the races that comprise the oppressed minorities of the United States. The majority of the people on our Pilgrimage are of Mexican descent, but the triumph of our race depends on a national association of all farm workers. The ranchers want to keep us divided in order to keep us weak. Many of us have signed individual "work contracts" with the ranchers or contractors, contracts in, which they had all the power. These contracts were farces, one more cynical joke at our impotence. That is why we must get together and bargain collectively. We must use the only strength that we have, the force of our numbers. The ranchers are few; we are many. UNITED WE SHALL STAND.

6. We will strike. We shall pursue the REVOLUTION we have proposed. We are sons of the Mexican Revolution, a revolution of the poor seeking bread and justice. Our revolution will not be armed, but we want the existing social order to dissolve; we want a new social order. We are poor, we are humble, and our only choice is to strike in those ranches where we are not treated with the respect we deserve as working men, where our rights as free and sovereign men are not recognized. We do not want the paternalism of the rancher, we do not want the contractor; we do not want charity at the price of our dignity. We want to be equal with all the working men in the nation; we want a just wage, better working conditions, a decent future for our children. To those who oppose us, be they ranchers, police, politicians, or speculators, we say that we are going to continue fighting until we die, or we win. WE SHALL OVERCOME. Across the San Joaquin Valley; across California, across the entire Southwest of the United States, wherever there are Mexican people, wherever there are farm workers, our movement is spreading like flames across a dry plain. Our PILGRIMAGE is the MATCH that will light our cause for all farm workers to see what is happening here, so that

they may do as we have done. The time has come for the liberation of the poor farm workers.

History is on our side.

MAY THE STRIKE GO ON! VIVA LA CAUSA!

Cesar Chavez, "The Plan of Delano," 1966. California Department of Education, Curriculum Frameworks and Instructional Resources, http://chavez.scientech.com.

DOCUMENT 5: PENITENCE AND REVOLUTION

*In this brief excerpt from a March 1966 fund-raising letter Chavez
appeals to the Mexican American community by characterizing
his march as an event that follows the traditions of Spanish religious culture and Mexican revolutionary history.*

In the "March from Delano to Sacramento" there is a meeting of
cultures and traditions; the centuries-old religious tradition of
Spanish culture conjoins with the very contemporary cultural
syndrome of "demonstration" springing from the spontaneity of
the poor, the downtrodden, the rejected, the discriminated-against
baring visibly their need and demand for equality and freedom.

In every religious oriented culture "the pilgrimage" has had a
place, a trip made with sacrifice and hardship as an expression
of penance and of commitment—and often involving a petition to
the patron of the pilgrimage for some sincerely sought benefit of
body or soul. . . .

The revolutions of Mexico were primarily uprisings of the
poor, fighting for bread and for dignity. The Mexican-American is
also a child of the revolution.

Pilgrimage, penance and revolution. The pilgrimage from Delano to Sacramento has strong religio-cultural overtones. But it is
also the pilgrimage of a cultural minority who have suffered from
a hostile environment and a minority who mean business.

Cesar Chavez, Fund-raising letter, March 1966. California Department of Education,
Curriculum Frameworks and Instructional Resources, http://chavez.scientech.com.

DOCUMENT 6: THE ETHICS OF COLLECTING DUES

*In 1966 Chavez and the National Farm Workers Association
(NFWA) met with sympathetic clergy to discuss fund-raising tactics, monthly dues, and other types of membership commitment.
This selection from the meeting highlights Chavez's moral argument behind asking for money from the poor.*

When we started organizing our union . . . there were people who
wanted to give us money. In fact one lady offered us $50,000 to or-
ganize workers. When I said, "No," she was very hurt. I told her,
"if I take the money now that would be the worst thing I could do.
I don't want the money. Some other time I will, but not now.". . .
The AFL-CIO had just spent a million and a half dollars and they

failed (to organize farm workers). So why did we think we could do it with $50,000. We started with (the principle that) no matter how poor the people, they had a responsibility to help the union. If they had $2.00 for food, they had to give $1.00 to the union. Otherwise, they would never get out of the trap of poverty. They would never have a union because they couldn't afford to sacrifice a little bit more on top of their misery. The statement, "they're so poor they can't afford to contribute to the group" is a great cop-out. You don't organize people by being afraid of them. You never have. You never will. You can be afraid of them in a variety of ways. But one of the main ways is to patronize them. You know the attitude: Blacks or browns or farm workers are so poor that they can't afford to (pay for) their own group. . . .

I went to a farm worker's home in McFarland, 7 miles south of Delano. It was winter. And there was no work. I knew it. And everyone knew it. As I knocked on the door, the guy in the little two-room house was going to the store with a $5.00 bill to get groceries. And there I was. He owed $7.00 because he was one full month behind plus the current one. So I'd come for $7.00. But all he had was $5.00. I had to make a decision. Should I take $3.50 or shouldn't I? It was very difficult. Up to this time I had been saying, "They should be paying. And if they don't pay they'll never have a union." $3.50 worth of food wasn't really going to change his life one way or the other that much. So I told him, "You have to pay at least $3.50 right now or I'll have to put you out of the union." He gave me the $5.00. We went to the store and changed the $5.00 bill. I got the $3.50 and gave him the $1.50. I stayed with him. He bought $1.50 worth of groceries and went home.

That experience hurt me but it also strengthened my determination. If this man was willing to give me $3.50 on a dream, when we were really taking the money out of his own food, then why shouldn't we be able to have a union—however difficult. There had never been a successful union for farm workers. Every . . . attempt had been defeated. People were killed. They ran into every obstacle you can think of. The whole agricultural industry along with government and business joined forces to break the unions and keep them from organizing. But with the kind of faith this farm worker had why couldn't we have a union?

So we set out to develop exactly that kind of faith. And by the time the strike came, we had that kind of resolution among members. Only a small percentage of the workers were paying dues. But it was ingrained in them that they were going to have a union come hell or high water. That's the kind of spirit that kept us going and infected other farm workers—this little core of people who were willing to stop talking and sacrifice to get it done.

Cesar Chavez, "Money and Organizing," *Social Policy*, vol. 32, no. 1, Fall 2001.

DOCUMENT 7: THE MEXICAN AMERICAN AND THE CHURCH

In 1968 Chavez wrote a speech titled "The Mexican-American and the Church" in which he describes the uneasy relationship between his farmworkers' unions and the Catholic Church. The first clergy supporters of La Causa were primarily Protestants from the Migrant Ministry while the farmworkers themselves were primarily Catholic. In the following passage Chavez argues that the time has come for Mexican American groups to pressure the Catholic Church for financial contributions from its well-endowed charity fund.

When poor people get involved in a long conflict, such as a strike, or a civil rights drive, and the pressure increases each day, there is a deep need for spiritual advice. Without it we see families crumble, leadership weaken, and hard workers grow tired. And in such a situation the spiritual advice must be given by a *friend*, not by part of the opposition. Thus, what sense does it make to go to Mass on Sunday and reach out for spiritual help, and instead get sermons about the wickedness of your cause. That only drives one to question and to despair. The growers in Delano have their spiritual problems; we do not deny that. They have every right to have priests and ministers who serve their needs. BUT WE HAVE DIFFERENT NEEDS, AND SO WE NEEDED A FRIENDLY SPIRITUAL GUIDE. And this is true in every community in this state where the poor face tremendous problems. . . .

The leadership of the Mexican-American Community must admit that we have fallen far short in our task of helping provide spiritual guidance for our people. We may say, "I don't feel any such need; I can get along." But that is a poor excuse for not helping provide such help for others. For we can also say, "I don't need any welfare help. I can take care of my own problems." But we are all willing to fight like hell for welfare aid for those who truly need it, who would starve without it. Likewise we may have gotten an education and not care about scholarship money for ourselves, or our children. But we would, we should, fight like hell to see to it that our state provides aid for any child needing it so that he can get the education he desires. LIKEWISE WE CAN SAY WE DON'T NEED THE CHURCH THAT IS OUR BUSINESS. BUT THERE ARE HUNDREDS OF THOUSANDS OF OUR PEOPLE WHO DESPERATELY NEED SOME HELP FROM THAT POWERFUL INSTITUTION, THE CHURCH, AND WE ARE FOOLISH NOT TO HELP THEM GET IT.

For example, the Catholic Charities agencies of the Catholic Church has millions of dollars earmarked for the poor. But often the money is spent for food baskets for the needy instead of for effective action to eradicate the causes of poverty. The men and women who administer this money sincerely want to help their brothers. It should be our duty to help direct the attention to the basic needs of the Mexican-Americans in our society—needs which cannot be satisfied with baskets of food, but rather with effective organizing at the grass roots level.

Therefore, I am calling the Mexican-American groups to stop ignoring this source of power. It is not just our right to appeal to the Church to use its power effectively for the poor, it is our duty to do so.

Cesar Chavez, "The Mexican-American and the Church," 1968. California Department of Education, Curriculum Frameworks and Instructional Resources, http://chavez. scientech.com.

DOCUMENT 8: CHRISTIAN PARTICIPATION

On February 14, 1968, Chavez began a fast for "penance and hope" that lasted for twenty-five days. In this letter dated February 20, 1968, Chavez asks for prayers and explains to the National Council of Churches his perception of their role in the Delano grape strike.

I have just begun the seventh day of a personal fast of penance and hope. After so many months of struggle and slow progress, I have become fearful that our common commitment to non-violence is weakening and that we may take dangerous shortcuts to victory. I accept full responsibility for this temptation and for all of its possible negative results. Our hope is the same as it has always been: that farm workers here can work together to change unjust conditions and thus to serve their brothers throughout the land.

My fast is informed by my religious faith and by my deep roots in the Church. It is not intended as a pressure on anyone but only as an expression of my own deep feelings and my own need to do penance and to be in prayer. I know you will understand and I ask that you pray for me.

I regret that I cannot be with you. . . . My own weakness and the crucial importance of non-violence for our struggle are the only things that could have kept me from your meeting. Please forgive me.

I would like to express the thanks of all Delano strikers for the early and faithful support of the churches. You have been with us from the beginning and at cost and we shall not forget it.

Our struggle in Delano is not over. In some ways it becomes more difficult each day. Our success (or failure) here and the quality of the organization we build will help us to shape the future for farm workers everywhere in our country. We do not take this responsibility lightly. But we cannot be faithful to this responsibility without the participation of the Christian community. You can help us survive and win new victories; but because of who you represent you can also help us stay true to our intention to serve our fellow farm workers.

We need and want your continued presence and support.

Winthrop Yinger, *Cesar Chavez: The Rhetoric of Nonviolence.* New York: Exposition Press, 1975.

DOCUMENT 9: STATEMENT OF THE FAST FOR NONVIOLENCE

Halfway through Chavez's twenty-five-day fast of February 1968, the United Farm Workers Organizing Committee AFL-CIO released this statement on the broader goals and implications of the fast. In it they emphasize Chavez's commitment to nonviolent sacrifice.

Cesar Chavez is engaged in a prolonged religious fast which is first and foremost a deeply personal act of penance and hope. But the personal nature of the fast does not limit it; rather, as all acts of love, Cesar's fast is for all men. Cesar's pain reminds us of the suffering of farm workers and of men of all races and kinds who are the victims of poverty and injustice. The hurt which he now accepts willingly points especially to the suffering that the Delano strikers bear as they struggle to achieve a better life for their fellow farm workers.

The fast is an act of penance, recalling farm workers to the nonviolent roots of their movement. These farm workers who are united in the Delano strike care about the well being of all fellow beings, even those who have placed themselves in the position of adversaries. They believe that these brothers can only be approached through determined creative and nonviolent means. If the commitment of nonviolence has been violated, in thought or deed, by himself, by the strikers, or by those who have rallied to the Cause, Cesar does penance.

The efforts to achieve justice through nonviolent sacrifice have achieved many important victories for the Delano strikers. Hopes of farm workers in all parts of the land have been raised by this sacrifice. Cesar's sacrifice recalls members of the farm workers' movement to the heavy responsibility of these hopes and aspirations. It is a powerful call for faithful and effective leadership so that present hopes will not turn to frustration, frustration to despair, despair to violence. It is a personal demand on each person to accept responsibility and to give the best of himself for a movement that is intent on setting other men free.

The fast points beyond the suffering of farm workers to the needs of the world. It is an act of the spirit which reaches to every man's need to escape living death and to begin giving of himself for the sake of other men. It is a personal act which beckons to each of us to participate in the nonviolent, worldwide struggle against man's inhumanity to man.

Winthrop Yinger, *Cesar Chavez: The Rhetoric of Nonviolence.* New York: Exposition Press, 1975.

DOCUMENT 10: GOD HELP US TO BE MEN

Chavez delivered this statement in March 1968 at the conclusion of his twenty-five-day fast for nonviolence. In it he reiterates his commitment to pacifism and ties it ideologically with machismo or "manliness." His audience consisted of thousands of farmworkers who had gathered in Delano to break the fast with their leader.

We are gathered here today not so much to observe the end of the Fast but because we are a family bound together in a common struggle for justice. We are a Union family celebrating our unity and the non-violent nature of our movement. Perhaps in the future we will come together at other times and places to break bread and to renew our courage and to celebrate important victories.

The Fast has had different meanings for different people. Some of you may still wonder about its meaning and importance. It was not intended as a pressure against any growers. For that reason we have suspended negotiations and arbitration proceedings and relaxed the militant picketing and boycotting of the strike during this period. I undertook this Fast because my heart was filled with grief and pain for the sufferings of farm workers. The Fast was first for me and then for all of us in this Union. It was a Fast for non-violence and a call to sacrifice.

Our struggle is not easy. Those who oppose our cause are rich and powerful and they have many allies in high places. We are poor. Our allies are few. But we have something the rich do not own. We have our own bodies and spirits and the justice of our cause as our weapons.

When we are really honest with ourselves we must admit that our lives are all that really belong to us. So, it is how we use our lives that determines what kind of men we are. It is my deepest belief that only by giving our lives do we find life. I am convinced that the truest act of courage, the strongest act of manliness is to sacrifice ourselves for others in a totally non-violent struggle for justice.

To be a man is to suffer for others. God help us to be men!

Cesar Chavez, Statement on the conclusion of a twenty-five-day fast for nonviolence, March 1968. California Department of Education, Curriculum Frameworks and Instructional Resources, http://chavez.scientech.com.

DOCUMENT 11: DETERMINATION AND FREEDOM

In this letter Chavez responds to an editorial piece written by E.L. Barr Jr., the president of the California Grape and Tree Fruit League, who accuses strikers of inciting violence. Chavez asks for proof of Mr. Barr's accusations and denies all charges. He pleads for freedom from agricultural enslavement through swift resolution of the strike.

Dear Mr. Barr,

I am sad to hear about your accusations in the press that our union movement and table grape boycott have been successful because we have used violence and terror tactics. If what you say is true, I have been a failure and should withdraw from the struggle. But you are left with the awesome moral responsibility, before God and man, to come forward with whatever information you have so that corrective action can begin at once.

If for any reason you fail to come forth to substantiate your charges then you must be held responsible for committing violence against us, albeit violence of the tongue. I am convinced that you as a human being did not mean what you said but rather acted hastily under pressure from the public relations firm that has been hired to try to counteract the tremendous moral force of our movement. How many times we ourselves have felt the need to lash out in anger and bitterness. . . .

By lying about the nature of our movement, Mr. Barr, you are working against nonviolent social change. Unwittingly perhaps, you may unleash that other force that our union by discipline and deed, censure and education has sought to avoid, that panacean short cut: that senseless violence that honors no color, class, or neighborhood. . . .

As your industry has experienced, our strikers here in Delano and those who represent us throughout the world are well trained for this struggle. They have been under the gun, they have been kicked and beaten and herded by dogs, they have been cursed and ridiculed, they have been stripped and chained and jailed, they have been sprayed with the poisons used in the vineyards. They have been taught not to lie down and die or to flee in shame, but to resist with every ounce of human endurance and spirit. To resist not with retaliation in kind but to overcome with love and compassion, with ingenuity and creativity, with hard work and longer hours, with stamina and patient tenacity, with truth and public appeal, with friends and allies, with mobility and discipline, with politics and law, and with prayer and fasting. They were not trained in a month or even a year; after all, this new harvest season will mark our fourth full year of strike and even now we continue to plan and prepare for the years to come. Time accomplishes for the poor what money does for the rich. . . .

Once again, I appeal to you as the representative of your industry and as a man. I ask you to recognize and bargain with our union before the economic pressure of the boycott and strike takes an irrevocable toll; but if not, I ask you to at least sit down with us to discuss the safeguards necessary to keep our historical struggle free of violence. I make this appeal because as one of the leaders of our nonviolent movement, I know and accept my responsibility for preventing, if possible, the destruction of human life and property. . . .

MR. BARR, let me be painfully honest with you. You must understand these things. We advocate militant nonviolence as our means for social revolution and to achieve justice for our people, but we are not blind or deaf to the desperate and moody winds of human frustration, impatience, and rage that blow among us. Gandhi himself admitted that if his only choices were cowardice or violence, he would choose violence. Men are not angels and the time and tides wait for no man. Precisely because of these powerful human emotions, we have tried to involve masses of people in their own struggle. Participation and self-determination remain the best experience of freedom; and free men instinctively prefer democratic change and even protect the rights guaranteed to seek it. Only the enslaved in despair have need of violent overthrow.

This letter does not express all that is in my heart, Mr. Barr. But if it says nothing else it says that we do not hate you or rejoice to see your industry destroyed; we hate the agribusiness system that seeks to keep us enslaved and we shall overcome and change it not by retaliation or bloodshed but by a determined nonviolent struggle carried on by those masses of farmworkers who intend to be free and human.

Sincerely yours, CESAR E. CHAVEZ

George D. Horowitz and Paul Fusco, *La Causa: The California Grape Strike.* New York: Macmillan, 1970.

DOCUMENT 12: AFTER THE STRIKE

The following selection is excerpted from the introduction to a book by Father Mark Day, a Roman Catholic priest who worked directly with the UFW during the crucial years of 1967–1970. On July 29, 1970, the UFWOC won contracts with all the major grape growers in the Delano area. In this excerpt, dated October 12, 1970, Chavez addresses the continuing relevance of the union.

I have always believed that, in order for any movement to be lasting, it must be built on the people. They must be the ones involved in forming it, and they must be the ones that ultimately control it. It is harder that way, but the benefits are more meaningful and lasting when won in this fashion. It is necessary to build a power base. Money by itself does not get the job done. This is why poverty programs have so much difficulty. Although many nice things are said and many wheels are spinning, very little real social change takes place. To try to change conditions without power is like trying to move a car without gasoline. If the workers are going to do anything, they need their own power. They need to involve themselves in meaningful ways. Once they achieve a victory, they can make use of their power to negotiate and change things for the better.

I have often been asked what kind of a union I am trying to

build and what type of society I want to see in the future. It seems to me that, once the union members are taken care of in terms of better wages and working conditions, the union must involve itself in the major issues of the times. The problem often arises that a group gets too involved in its own successes and doesn't have time for anything else. It is my hope that we keep ourselves focused on our ideals. It is much easier to profess something by words and not by deeds. Our job, then, is to educate our members so that they will be conscious of the needs of others less fortunate than themselves. The scope of the worker's interest must motivate him to reach out and help others. If we can get across the idea of participating in other causes, then we have real education.

As for the nation as a whole, it doesn't matter to me how our government is structured or what type of political party one may have. The real change comes about when men really want it. In a small way we try to change ourselves and we try to change those with whom we come into contact. You can't organize the masses unless you organize individuals. I like to think of our group as a "doer" type union. We place a great deal of emphasis on doing things and very little on theorizing or writing about them. . . .

We must be vitally concerned about educating people to the significance of peace and nonviolence as positive forces in our society. But our concern must not be frozen on a highly sophisticated level. We are concerned with peace, because violence (and war is the worst type of violence) has no place in our society or in our world, and it must be eradicated. Next to union contracts, we must focus our attention to bring about the necessary changes in our society through nonviolent means. We must train effective organizers for this purpose.

We must acquaint people with peace—not because capitalism is better or communism is better, but because, as men, we are better. As men we don't want to kill anyone, and we don't want to be killed ourselves. We must reach everyone so that this message can go out. If we do this correctly, our people will rise above mere material interests and goals. They will become involved in cultural matters. And we need a cultural revolution among ourselves—not only in art but also in the realm of the spirit. As poor people and immigrants, all of us have brought to this country some very important things of the spirit. But too often they are choked, they are not allowed to flourish in our society.

People are not going to turn back now. The poor are on the march: black, brown, red, everyone, whites included. We are now in the midst of the biggest revolution this country has ever known. It really doesn't matter, in the final analysis, how powerful we are, how many boycotts we win, how many growers we sign up, or how much political clout we possess, if in the process we forget whom we are serving. We must never forget that the human element is the most important thing we have—if we get away from this, we are certain to fail.

Mark Day, *Forty Acres: Cesar Chavez and the Farmworkers.* New York: Praeger, 1971.

DOCUMENT 13: STATEMENT FROM PHOENIX

In early 1972 the UFW mobilized politically. They protested Arizona Proposition 22, a measure that would have outlawed boycotting, and campaigned for recall of Governor Jack Williams. From May 12 to June 4, 1972, Chavez fasted to attract attention to these and other UFW efforts. The statement he released at the end of his "24-Day Fast for Justice," part of which is excerpted here, contains the quote: "What a terrible irony it is that the very people who harvest the food we eat do not have enough food for their own children."

I am weak in my body but I feel very strong in my spirits. I am happy to end the fast because it is not an easy thing. But it is also not easy for my family and for many of you who have worried and worked and sacrificed. The Fast was meant as a call to sacrifice for justice and as a reminder of how much suffering there is among farm workers. In fact, what is a few days without food in comparison to the daily pain of our brothers and sisters who do backbreaking work in the fields under inhuman conditions and without hope of ever breaking their cycle of poverty and misery. What a terrible irony it is that the very people who harvest the food we eat do not have enough food for their own children.

It is possible to become discouraged about the injustice we see everywhere. But God did not promise us that the world would be humane and just. He gives us the gift of life and allows us to choose the way we will use our limited time on this earth. It is an awesome opportunity. We should be thankful for the life we have been given, thankful for the opportunity to do something about the suffering of our fellowman. We can choose to use our lives for others to bring about a better and more just world for our children. People who make that choice will know hardship and sacrifice. But if you give yourself totally to the non-violent struggle for peace and justice, you also find that people will give you their hearts and you will never go hungry and never be alone. And in giving of yourself you will discover a whole new life full of meaning and love. . . .

Our opponents in the agricultural industry are very powerful and farm workers are still weak in money and influence. But we have another kind of power that comes from the justice of our cause. So long as we are willing to sacrifice for that cause, so long as we persist in non-violence and work to spread the message of our struggle, then millions of people around the world will respond from their hearts, will support our efforts . . . and in the end we will overcome. It can be done. We know it can be done. God give us the strength and patience to do it without bitterness so that we can win both our friends and opponents to the cause of justice.

Cesar Chavez, "Statement at the End of His 24-Day Fast for Justice," June 1972. California Department of Education, Curriculum Frameworks and Instructional Resources, http://chavez.scientech.com.

DOCUMENT 14: ON MARTIN LUTHER KING AND NONVIOLENCE

Chavez titled his 1978 tribute to Martin Luther King Jr. "He Showed Us the Way." He credits the late civil rights leader with philosophically and strategically influencing the farmworkers' movement. On the anniversary of King's death Chavez elaborates on the moral and historical arguments against violence.

In honoring Martin Luther King, Jr.'s memory we also acknowledge nonviolence as a truly powerful weapon to achieve equality and liberation—in fact, the only weapon that Christians who struggle for social change can claim as their own.

Dr. King's entire life was an example of power that nonviolence brings to bear in the real world. It is an example that inspired much of the philosophy and strategy of the farm workers' movement. This observance of Dr. King's death gives us the best possible opportunity to recall the principles with which our struggle has grown and matured. . . .

We are . . . convinced that nonviolence is more powerful than violence. Nonviolence supports you if you have a just and moral cause. . . .

The greater the oppression, the more leverage nonviolence holds. Violence does not work in the long run and if it is temporarily successful, it replaces one violent form of power with another just as violent. People suffer from violence. Examine history. Who gets killed in the case of violent revolution? The poor, the workers. The people of the land are the ones who give their bodies and don't really gain that much for it. We believe it is too big a price to pay for not getting anything. Those who espouse violence exploit people. To call men to arms with many promises, to ask them to give up their lives for a cause and then not produce for them afterwards, is the most vicious type of oppression.

We know that most likely we are not going to do anything else the rest of our lives except build our union. For us there is nowhere else to go. Although we would like to see victory come soon, we are willing to wait. In this sense time is our ally. We learned many years ago that the rich may have money, but the poor have time.

It has been our experience that few men or women ever have the opportunity to know the true satisfaction that comes with giving one's life totally in the nonviolent struggle for justice. Martin Luther King, Jr., was one of these unique servants and from him we learned many of the lessons that have guided us. For these lessons and for his sacrifice for the poor and oppressed, Dr. King's memory will be cherished in the hearts of the farm workers forever.

Cesar Chavez, "Tribute to Martin Luther King Jr.," April 1978. California Department of Education, Curriculum Frameworks and Instructional Resources, http://chavez. scientech.com.

DOCUMENT 15: DARK FORCES AND ENEMIES

In the early 1980s, as membership in the UFW began its decline, Chavez found himself facing philosophical divisions within upper union management and external legal battles with agribusiness and the Agricultural Labor Relations Board (ALRB). When he addressed the UFW constitutional convention in September 1984 Chavez railed against California governor Deukmejian whose appointees to the ALRB had rendered it largely ineffectual. In his speech he predicts that the only escape from the shadows of reactionary politics will come when people of color are the majority voting bloc.

There is a shadow falling over the land, brothers and sisters, and the dark forces of reaction threaten us now as never before.

The enemies of the poor and the working classes hold power in the White House and the governor's office.

Our enemies seek to impose a new Bracero program on the farm workers of America—they seek to return to the days—before there was a farm workers union—when our people were treated as if they were agricultural implements instead of human beings.

Our enemies seek to hand over millions of dollars in government money to segregated private colleges that close their doors to blacks and other people of color.

Our enemies have given the wealthiest people the biggest tax cuts in American history at the same time they have increased taxes for the poor and working people.

They have created a whole new class of millionaires while forcing millions of ordinary people into poverty. . . .

Our enemies want all of us to carry identification cards issued by the government which only we will be forced to produce to get a job to apply for unemployment insurance—to keep from being deported by the border patrol. . . .

Our enemies are responsible for the brutal murder of thousands of dark-skinned, Spanish-speaking farm workers through their military support of blood-thirsty dictators in Central America. The men, women and children who have been slaughtered committed the same crimes we have committed—they wanted a better life for themselves and their families—a life free from hunger and poverty and exploitation.

The same dark forces of reaction which dominate the government in Washington also dominate the government in Sacramento. . . .

What does all this mean for you and for other farm workers?

It means that the right to vote in free elections is a sham!

It means that the right to talk freely about the union among your fellow workers on the job is a cruel hoax.

It means the right to be free from threats and intimidation by growers is an empty promise.

It means the right to sit down and negotiate with your employer as equals across the bargaining table—and not as peons in the fields—is a fraud. . . .

The day will come when we're the majority when our children are the lawyers and the doctors and the politicians—when we hold political power in this state.

These trends are part of the forces of history that cannot be stopped. No governor and no organization of rich growers can resist them for very long. They are inevitable.

Once change begins, it cannot be stopped. You cannot uneducate the person who has learned to read.

You cannot humiliate the person who feels pride.

You cannot oppress the people who are not afraid anymore.

Our people are on the move. Our day is coming. It may not come this year. It may not come during this decade. But it will come, someday!

Cesar Chavez, "Address to UFW's 7th Constitutional Convention," September 1984. California Department of Education, Curriculum Frameworks and Instructional Resources, http://chavez.scientech.com.

DOCUMENT 16: CHILD LABOR AND OTHER CATASTROPHES

In his November 9, 1984, address to the Commonwealth Club of California, Chavez opens with the grim state of worker life in the fields. Although the tone is pessimistic, he remains convinced that a farm labor revolution is inevitable.

Twenty-one years ago last September, on a lonely stretch of railroad track paralleling U.S. Highway 101 near Salinas, 32 Bracero farm workers lost their lives in a tragic accident.

The Braceros had been imported from Mexico to work on California farms. They died when their bus, which was converted from a flatbed truck, drove in front of a freight train. Conversion of the bus had not been approved by any government agency. The driver had "tunnel" vision.

Most of the bodies lay unidentified for days. No one, including the grower who employed the workers, even knew their names.

Today, thousands of farm workers live under savage conditions—beneath trees and amid garbage and human excrement—near tomatoe fields in San Diego County, tomatoe fields which use the most modern farm technology.

Vicious rats gnaw on them as they sleep. They walk miles to buy food at inflated prices. And they carry in water from irrigation pumps.

Child labor is still common in many farm areas.

As much as 30 percent of Northern California's garlic harvesters are under-aged children. Kids as young as six years old have voted in state-conducted union elections since they qualified as workers. Some 800,000 under-aged children work with their families harvesting crops across America. Babies born to migrant workers suffer 25 percent higher infant mortality than the rest of the population.

Malnutrition among migrant worker children is 10 times higher than the national rate. Farm workers' average life expectancy is still 49 years—compared to 73 years for the average American.

All my life, I have been driven by one dream, one goal, one vision: To overthrow a farm labor system in this nation which treats farm workers as if they were not important human beings.

Cesar Chavez, "Address by Cesar Chavez, President, United Farm Workers of America, AFL-CIO, The Commonwealth Club of California, November 9, 1984—San Francisco." Cesar E. Chavez Institute for Public Policy, San Francisco State University, www.sfsu.edu.

DOCUMENT 17: FAST TO PROTEST PESTICIDES

Sounding hopeful for the future of the farmworkers' movement, Chavez thanks the Kennedys and all his supporters at the end of his 1988 fast to protest pesticide poisoning. He expresses the wish that others will fast in solidarity with the movement and its social and environmental goals.

My heart is too full and my body too weak to read this message. So I have asked my oldest son, Fernando, to read it to you.

I thank God for the love and support of my family as well as for the prayers and hard work of the members and staff of our Union. I am grateful to the many thousands of people who came to be with me and for the millions who have kept me in their prayers and who have taken up our cause in their own communities. They have opened up their hearts, not just to me, but to the farm workers and the families who suffer from the unrestrained poisoning of our soil, our water, our air and our people.

Many generous people have traveled long distances to be here during the fast. It is especially meaningful to me and all farm workers to have Ethel Kennedy and her children here on this day.

Twenty years ago Bobby Kennedy stood with us when few had the courage to do so. We will always carry him in our hearts.

Today I pass on the fast for life to hundreds of concerned men and women throughout North America and the world who have offered to share the suffering. They will help carry the burden by continuing the fast in front of their local supermarkets.

The fast will go on in hundreds of distant places and it will multiply among thousands and then millions of caring people until every poisoned grape is off the supermarket shelves. And the fast will endure until the fields are safe for farm workers, the environment is preserved for future generations, and our food is once again a source of nourishment and life.

"Cesar Chavez's Statement at the End of the Fast, August 21, 1988." California Department of Education, Curriculum Frameworks and Instructional Resources, http://chavez.scientech.com.

DOCUMENT 18: ENVIRONMENTAL POISONS

At the end of the 1980s the focus for Chavez and the UFW became the battle against abuses of pesticides that had caused cancer and birth defects in worker populations. In this speech delivered to Pacific Lutheran University in March 1989 Chavez alerts his audience to safety problems affecting both farmworkers and consumers.

What is the worth of a man or a woman? What is the worth of a farm worker? How do you measure the value of a life?

Ask the parents of Johnnie Rodriguez.

Johnnie Rodriguez was not even a man; Johnnie was a five year old boy when he died after a painful two year battle against cancer.

His parents, Juan and Elia, are farm workers. Like all grape workers, they are exposed to pesticides and other agricultural chemicals. Elia worked in the table grapes around Delano, California until she was eight months pregnant with Johnnie.

Juan and Elia cannot say for certain if pesticides caused their son's cancer. But neuroblastoma is one of the cancers found in McFarland, a small farm town only a few miles from Delano, where the Rodriguezes live. . . .

Johnnie Rodriguez was one of 13 McFarland children diagnosed with cancer in recent years; and one of six who have died from the disease. With only 6,000 residents, the rate of cancer in McFarland is 400 percent above normal.

In McFarland and in Fowler childhood cancer cases are being reported in excess of expected rates. In Delano and other farming towns, questions are also being raised.

The chief source of carcinogens in these communities are pesticides from the vineyards and fields that encircle them. Health experts believe the high rate of cancer in McFarland is from pesticides and nitrate-containing fertilizers leaching into the water system from surrounding fields. . . .

Our critics sometimes ask, "why should the United Farm Workers worry about pesticides when farm workers have so many other more obvious problems?"

The wealth and plenty of California agribusiness are built atop the suffering of generations of California farm workers. Farm labor history across America is one shameful tale after another of hardship and exploitation.

Malnutrition among migrant children. Tuberculosis, pneumonia and respiratory infections. Average life expectancy more than twenty years below the U.S. norm.

Savage living conditions. Miserable wages and working conditions. Sexual harassment of women workers. Widespread child labor. Inferior schools or no school at all. . . .

For 100 years succeeding waves of immigrants have sweated and sacrificed to make this industry rich. And for their sweat and for their sacrifice, farm workers have been repaid with humiliation and contempt. With all these problems, why, then, do we dwell so on the perils of pesticides?

Because there is something even more important to farm workers than the benefits unionization brings.

Because there is something more important to the farm workers' union than winning better wages and working conditions.

That is protecting farm workers—and consumers—from systematic poisoning through the reckless use of agricultural toxics.

There is nothing we care more about than the lives and safety of our families.

Cesar Chavez, "Address by Cesar Chavez, President, United Farm Workers of America, AFL-CIO, March 1989, Tacoma, Washington, Pacific Lutheran University." Cesar E. Chavez Institute for Public Policy, San Francisco State University, www.sfsu.edu.

DOCUMENT 19: AWARDED THE PRESIDENTIAL MEDAL OF FREEDOM

These remarks are excerpted from President Bill Clinton's August 8, 1994, speech on the presentation of the Presidential Medal of Freedom to the late Cesar Chavez. At the ceremony Helen Chavez accepted the award on his behalf.

Thank you very much. Ladies and gentlemen, welcome to the White House. As you might imagine, one of the great pleasures of the presidency is selecting recipients of the Presidential Medal of Freedom—the highest honor given to civilians by the United States of America. . . .

Cesar Chavez, before his death in April of last year, had become a champion of working people everywhere. Born into Depression-era poverty in Arizona in 1927, he served in the United States Navy in the second world war, and rose to become one of our greatest advocates of nonviolent change. He was for his own people a Moses figure.

The farm workers who labored in the fields and yearned for respect and self-sufficiency pinned their hopes on this remarkable man, who, with faith and discipline, with soft-spoken humility and amazing inner strength, led a very courageous life. And in so doing, brought dignity to the lives of so many others, and provided for us inspiration for the rest of our nation's history.

We are honored to have his wife, friend and long-time working partner, Helen Chavez, to be with us today to receive the award. . . .

Ladies and gentlemen, in closing let me say that I couldn't help thinking as the citations were read and I looked into the faces of our honorees and their families, friends and admirers here, that we too often reserve our greatest accolades for our citizens when they are gone. I wish that Cesar Chavez could be here today.

William Clinton, "August 8, 1994, Remarks by the President in Medal of Freedom Ceremony," www.sfsu.edu.

DISCUSSION QUESTIONS

CHAPTER 1

1. When Cesar Chavez was a child, he and his family were dispossessed of their home and struggled to find migrant work. According to Jan Young, what values did Chavez learn from this experience? How might these events have impacted Chavez's attitudes toward community organizing and social justice?

2. Jean Maddern Pitrone writes in evocative, often radical language about migrant life. How does he describe migrant farmworker life as experienced by the Chavez family? Do the author's sentiments seem exaggerated due to his obvious admiration of Chavez? Cite examples from the text in your response.

3. According to Andrew Kopkind, why did Cesar Chavez decide that a strike in the vineyards of Delano would benefit farmworkers? What did Chavez hope to accomplish by striking? What was his vision of success for the farmworkers?

CHAPTER 2

1. Jacques E. Levy chronicles episodes of violence faced by Chavez supporters and workers on the picket line. In your opinion, why was nonviolent protest important to Cesar Chavez? How did Chavez's philosophy of nonviolence affect the development of the United Farm Workers (UFW)?

2. Given that Cesar Chavez and the UFW had to fight for such essentials as potable water and bathroom facilities, what challenges did Chavez face in his efforts to build a lasting farmworkers' union? According to the articles by Jacques E. Levy and Mark Day, what types of hostilities confronted Chavez personally?

CHAPTER 3

1. Fred Ross colorfully recalls his relationship with Chavez during their first years of involvement with the Commu-

nity Service Organization (CSO). According to Ross, what attributes did Chavez display as an organizer for the CSO? How would you characterize the relationship between Ross and Chavez? What or who persuaded Cesar Chavez to become a union organizer? Explain your answer.

2. John C. Hammerback, Richard J. Jensen, and Jose Angel Gutierrez argue that a large part of Cesar Chavez's success can be attributed to his mastery of effective public speaking. In the authors' opinion, what were some of the characteristics of Chavez's speeches? How did Chavez present himself to his audience? What problems did Cesar Chavez address in his speeches?

3. Along with nonviolence, Cesar Chavez stressed the importance of worker solidarity and cultural egalitarianism. Historians Matt S. Meier and Feliciano Rivera describe Cesar Chavez's role in history as a Chicano leader. In your opinion, is it appropriate or does it do Chavez a disservice to characterize him as a Latino leader? Defend your response.

Chapter 4

1. When Cesar Chavez died, thousands mourned, including activist Frank Bardacke. In his controversial article, how does Bardacke assess the legacy of Cesar Chavez? Considering the continuing problems faced by migrant workers and the currently reduced membership of the UFW, in your opinion, how successful was Cesar Chavez? Explain your reasoning.

2. In the years since the death of Cesar Chavez there have been hundreds of school, street, and civic rededications in his name. Richard Griswold del Castillo and Richard A. Garcia list several ways that Chavez influenced American history. What were Chavez's main accomplishments in the authors' view? In your opinion, has Chavez received too much recognition for his efforts or not enough?

3. Do you believe farm laborers would have been capable of improving their living conditions without Cesar Chavez? In other words, did the farmworkers need him? Why or why not? Use readings to support your conclusion.

CHRONOLOGY

1927

On March 31, Cesar Estrada Chavez is born to Librado and Juana Estrada Chavez on an Arizona farm.

1929

On October 24, the crash of the stock market precipitates the worldwide financial catastrophe known as the Great Depression. Unemployment reaches staggering levels; many head west in search of work.

1931

Severe drought plagues fields in the southern and western United States; dust storms increase and crops are destroyed. Displaced laborers from the "Dust Bowl" head west looking for work. A massive pool of unemployed laborers competes for jobs as migrant workers.

1935

The National Labor Relations Act is passed, guaranteeing workers organizing and collective bargaining rights.

1937

On August 29, the Chavez property is repossessed after the family defaults on a bank loan. The Chavez family loses their home, farm, and grocery store.

1939

The Chavezes leave Arizona and find work as migrant laborers. The severe national drought ends in the fall.

1941

On December 7, after the Japanese bombing of Pearl Harbor, the United States enters World War II. The war effort drains the pool of available laborers for farmwork.

1942

After Librado is injured in a car accident, young Cesar Chavez is forced to quit school to help support the family.

They work seasonal crops such as lettuce fields. Congress enacts the Bracero Program to fill vacancies in agricultural jobs.

1943

The Chavez family relocates to Delano, California.

1944

Cesar Chavez violates the "whites only" segregation in a movie theater and is arrested. He joins the navy and serves in the Pacific fleet.

1946

Chavez receives his discharge from the navy and returns to Delano to work in the vineyards.

1948

On October 22, Chavez marries Helen Fabela.

1952

Fred Ross recruits Chavez into Saul Alinsky's Community Service Organization (CSO). Chavez holds house meetings and voter registration drives.

1958

The CSO promotes Chavez to general director.

1959

Chavez begins his lifelong relationship with Robert Kennedy after they meet to discuss issues such as voter registration drives.

1960

On February 1, sit-ins are held in Greensboro, North Carolina, to protest segregation. On April 15, the Student Nonviolent Coordinating Committee is established to organize civil rights protesters. In November, CBS airs "Harvest of Shame," a documentary on the squalid living conditions of farm laborers in the United States.

1962

On March 31, Chavez resigns from the CSO in a dispute over the organization's unwillingness to charter a union specifically for farmworkers. Activist Dolores Huerta joins him. On September 30, Chavez and Huerta create the National Farm Workers Association (NFWA), where they unveil the eagle flag and the slogan *¡Si Se Puede!* ("Yes, we can!").

1965

On September 8, Larry Itilong's Agricultural Workers Organizing Committee (AWOC) strikes in the vineyards of Delano to protest low wages and oppressive working conditions. On September 16, Mexican Independence Day, Chavez's NFWA joins the effort and the Great Delano Grape Strike is undertaken. The Bracero Program is officially ended.

1966

On March 16, Chavez leads supporters on a march to the state capital, Sacramento, to draw attention to the Great Delano Grape Strike. The NFWA and AWOC unions merge to form the United Farm Workers of America (UFW) with Chavez named director. Chavez fasts for thirteen days to pray for victory in the ongoing conflicts for worker jurisdiction with the Teamsters. Robert Kennedy holds hearings regarding violence against striking workers in Delano.

1967

The UFW union creates a central office complex known as "Forty Acres" in Delano.

1968

On February 14, Chavez fasts for twenty-five days to draw attention to the grape strike. Senator Robert Kennedy breaks the fast with Chavez. On April 4, Martin Luther King Jr. is assassinated. On June 5, Robert Kennedy is assassinated.

1969

On May 10, Chavez marches in Indio, California. Jacques E. Levy begins his reporter's notebook on Chavez.

1970

On July 29, contracts with the Giumarra Vineyards and twenty-seven other growers are signed. Chavez targets Bud Antle Lettuce. On December 14, Chavez is jailed in Salinas, California, as a result of the lettuce boycott; he is released in ten days.

1971

Chavez and the UFW acquire a converted tuberculosis sanatorium and create a new headquarters near Keene, California. They name it "La Paz."

1972

Proposition 22, which would outlaw boycotts, is defeated. In April, Chavez fasts for twenty-four days in Phoenix. The

American Federation of Labor and Congress of Industrial Organizations (AFL-CIO) charters the UFW.

1973

Bloody turf wars continue between the UFW and the Teamsters. The UFW holds a convention in Fresno at which a UFW constitution is ratified. On June 27, to protest clandestine dealings with the Teamsters Union, Chavez announces a strike on the Gallo Vineyards.

1975

On February 22, the Gallo boycott is energized with a march on Modesto, California. In May, the California Agricultural Labor Relations Act passes, and the Agricultural Labor Relations Board is formed.

1977

A truce is signed between the UFW and the Teamsters.

1978

The Gallo boycott ends.

1979

Several prominent members leave the UFW, and Chavez orders an internal restructuring.

1984

Chavez and the UFW declare a new boycott on grapes.

1987

The Wrath of Grapes, a movie about the pesticide poisoning of workers, is produced by the UFW. Chavez screens the movie across the country.

1988

On July 16, Chavez fasts for thirty-six days to protest the use of pesticides. Jesse Jackson attends the break of the fast.

1990

On November 12, Chavez is awarded the Aztec Eagle, the highest civilian honor, from the president of Mexico.

1991

The UFW is ordered to pay $5.4 million to a lettuce grower, Bruce Church, Inc., for boycott damages.

1992

Chavez leads a march through the Coachella and San Joaquin valleys to protest low wages.

1993

Chavez travels to Arizona to testify in the Bruce Church court case. On April 23, while in Arizona, Chavez dies in his sleep. More than forty thousand people take part in the funeral procession. Pope John II telegraphs his condolences.

1994

President Bill Clinton posthumously awards Cesar Chavez the Presidential Medal of Freedom; his wife, Helen, accepts it on his behalf. California governor Pete Wilson declares March 31 a state holiday in honor of Cesar Chavez.

FOR FURTHER RESEARCH

SPEECHES AND WRITINGS BY CESAR CHAVEZ

Richard J. Jensen and John C. Hammerback, eds., *The Words of Cesar Chavez*. College Station: Texas A&M University Press, 2002.

Jacques E. Levy, *Cesar Chavez: An Autobiography of La Causa*. New York: Norton, 1975.

BIOGRAPHIES OF CESAR CHAVEZ

Mark Day, *Forty Acres: Cesar Chavez and the Farm Workers*. New York: Praeger, 1971.

Richard W. Etulain, ed. *Cesar Chavez: A Brief Biography with Documents*. Boston: Bedford/St. Martin's, 2002.

Richard Griswold del Castillo and Richard A. Garcia, *Cesar Chavez: A Triumph of Spirit*. Norman: University of Oklahoma Press, 1995.

Susan Ferriss and Ricardo Sandoval, *The Fight in the Fields: Cesar Chavez and the Farmworkers Movement*. New York: Harcourt Brace, 1997.

John C. Hammerback, Richard J. Jensen, and Jose Angel Gutierrez, *The Rhetorical Career of Cesar Chavez*. College Station: Texas A&M University Press, 1998.

Joan London and Henry Anderson, *So Shall Ye Reap*. New York: Crowell, 1970.

Peter Matthiessen, *Sal Si Puedes: Cesar Chavez and the New American Revolution*. New York: Dell, 1969.

Matt S. Meier and Feliciano Rivera, *The Chicanos: A History of Mexican Americans*. New York: Hill and Wang, 1972.

Jean Maddern Pitrone, *Chavez: Man of the Migrants*. New York: Alba House, 1971.

Fred Ross, *Conquering Goliath: Cesar Chavez at the Beginning.* Keene, CA: El Taller Grafico Press, 1989.

Ronald B. Taylor, *Chavez and the Farm Workers.* Boston: Beacon Press, 1975.

James P. Terzian, *Mighty Hard Road: The Story of Cesar Chavez.* New York: Doubleday, 1970.

Jan Young, *The Migrant Workers and Cesar Chavez.* New York: Messner, 1972.

GENERAL INFORMATION ON CHAVEZ AND THE UNITED FARM WORKERS

Rudolfo A. Anaya, *An Elegy on the Death of Cesar Chavez.* El Paso: Cinco Puntos Press, 2000.

Cletus E. Daniel, *Bitter Harvest: A History of California Farmworkers, 1870–1941.* Berkeley and Los Angeles: University of California Press, 1981.

———, *Labor Leaders in America.* Ed. Melvyn Dubofsky and Warren Van Tine. Chicago: University of Illinois Press, 1987.

Dana De Ruiz, *La Causa: The Migrant Farmworkers' Story.* Austin, TX: Raintree Steck-Vaughn, 1993.

Susan Samuels Drake, *Fields of Courage: Remembering Cesar Chavez and the People Whose Labor Feeds Us.* Santa Cruz, CA: Many Names Press, 1999.

John Gregory Dunne, *Delano: The Story of the California Grape Strike.* New York: Farrar, Straus & Giroux, 1967.

Beverly Fodell, *Cesar Chavez and the United Farm Workers: A Selective Bibliography.* Detroit, MI: Wayne State University Press, 1974.

Ernesto Galarza, *Strangers in Our Fields.* Washington, DC: Joint United States–Mexico Trade Union Committee, 1956.

David G. Gutiérrez, *Walls and Mirrors: Mexican Americans, Mexican Immigrants, and the Politics of Ethnicity.* Berkeley: University of California Press, 1995.

Pat Hoffman, *Ministry of the Dispossessed: Learning from the Farm Worker Movement.* Los Angeles: Wallace Press, 1987.

Sam Kushner, *Long Road to Delano.* New York: International Publishers, 1975.

David R. Maciel and Isidro D. Ortiz, eds., *Chicanas/Chicanos at the Crossroads: Social, Economic, and Political Change.* Tuscon: University of Arizona Press, 1996.

Ann McGregor, comp., and Cindy Wathen, ed., *Remembering Cesar: The Legacy of Cesar Chavez.* Clovis, CA: Quill Driver Books, 2000.

Rick Tejada-Flores and Ray Telles, *The Fight In the Fields: Cesar Chavez and the Fieldworkers' Struggle* [video]. St. Paul, MN: Independent Television Service, 1996.

Winthrop Yinger, *Cesar Chavez: The Rhetoric of Nonviolence.* New York: Exposition Press, 1975.

INDEX